# NEVER TRUST A COWBIRD

BY THE SAME AUTHOR

*Never Pet a Porcupine*

George
Laycock

# *Never*
# *Trust*
# *a Cowbird*

W · W · Norton & Company · Inc ·

*New York*

ACKNOWLEDGEMENTS: The author wishes to express his appreciation to the editors and publishers of the following publications for their kind permission to include in this book stories which first appeared in their periodicals: *Field and Stream,* Holt, Rinehart, and Winston; *IH Farm,* farm publication of the International Harvester Company; *Ford Times,* Ford Motor Company.

CREDITS: Photographs of mule, guinea fowl, ant, cotton boll weevil—U. S. Department of Agriculture. Black vulture, red-winged blackbird, cowbird, big brown bat, screech owl, pileated woodpecker—Karl Maslowski. Crawfish—Arkansas Game and Fish Commission. Goat, border collie—Joe Munroe, *Farm Quarterly.* All other photographs by the author.

# CONTENTS

1   *Never Trust a Cowbird*                          13
2   *Consider the Mule*                              21
3   *Barnyard Extrovert*                             27
4   *The Famous Hopper*                              33
5   *The Shepherd's Best Friend*                     39
6   *The Antique Cattle*                             43
7   *Pigeon Talk*                                    49
8   *Crawfish Have Their Troubles*                   55
9   *The Untidy Ones*                                63
10  *Congratulate the Redwing*                       73
11  *Over the Hills with the Foxhounds*              81
12  *Watchbird in the Barnyard*                      85
13  *See No Weevil*                                  91
14  *Honking Watchdog*                               97
15  *Owl, They Say, That Screeches*                 103
16  *The Determined Ant*                            111
17  *Powerful Woodpecker*                           119
18  *The Unlovely Bat*                              129

# ILLUSTRATIONS

| | |
|---|---|
| Cowbird | *12* |
| Mule | *20* |
| Goat | *26* |
| Grasshopper | *32* |
| Border Collie | *38* |
| Longhorns | *44-45* |
| Pigeon | *50* |
| Crawfish | *54* |
| Vulture | *65* |
| Red-winged Blackbird | *75* |
| Foxhound | *80* |
| Guinea fowl | *87* |
| Boll Weevil | *93* |
| Goose | *99* |
| Screech Owl | *102* |
| Ant | *110* |
| Pileated Woodpecker | *118* |
| Bat | *128* |

# ANIMALS WE SEE

As the white man advanced across the continent, he altered forever the world the native wild animals knew. Gone were marshes, forests and prairie grasses. In their places stood farms, villages and concrete highways. The changes that came to the face of the land forced some animals to live near the haunts of man. Some lived even better than before. Others, unable to adjust, dwindled with the ever-shrinking wilderness. Some disappeared forever.

With him, when he settled the land, the white man brought his own animals to enrich his life. All of his domesticated animals, dogs, horses, goats, sheep, swine, cattle and fowl, came, in some ancient age, from wild ancestors.

The animals in this book, wild or domesticated, native or foreign, are from the world of common animals we see today. Some are in the towns. Some are in the barnyards. Some are in the woods and fields. But all are part of the animal community as men have remodeled it. Each of these familiar animals, sharing the changing world with men, has its own interesting story—the story of its life and how it gets along with people.

*George Laycock*
*April, 1965*

# NEVER TRUST A COWBIRD

# ONE

# *Never Trust a Cowbird*

Of all the birds in North America, the cowbird is the only one that knows how to perpetuate his race without tying himself down. The female cowbird furtively slips through the woods and weeds, and leaves her eggs in the nests of other, usually smaller, birds. And then she lets her neighbors rear her young while she and her mate go through the summer months living life to the fullest. They dance but do not pay the fiddler.

The cowbird is a small blackbird. The male has a drab brown head and a glossy body, while the female is uniformly gray, dull colors indeed for a pair leading such a gay life.

You'll see them with flocks of other blackbirds.

And you'll know them by their smaller size. Or you'll see them in the pastures around the cows, for here they find food in abundance. Cowbirds feed on insects the cows kick up from the grass.

When he grows weary of feeding on the ground, the cowbird, in his carefree fashion, may flit to the back of a cow and ride at peace with the world while picking up any insect that ventures near. When the West was young he was the constant companion of the buffalo and was called buffalo bird.

There comes a time in any bird's life when duty calls. With the female cowbird the duty may be light but the call is strong. In spring and early summer she must locate baby sitters. Her methods are more than happenstance.

She keeps her beady little eyes open to discover where other birds are building their nests. There are days when a red-eyed vireo with a beak full of grass holds more fascination for the female cowbird than a peck of green worms. She will follow the vireo at a distance until she locates the nest.

Some strange alchemy within her more often than not brings the development of her egg at the right time for the nest. But she must take care not to rush things. If her egg is the first one in the nest, the vireo will abandon. Apparently the vireo can count to one but not to two.

The yellow warbler victimized by a cowbird often builds a second floor over the egg and starts again.

They have been known to build five-story nests. To some observers. this is ample evidence that birds have the power to reason.

Cowbirds often remove an egg from the host's nest before leaving one of their own. This theft usually occurs the day before the cowbird leaves her own treasure in the nest. The female cowbird opens her beak, punctures the egg, and flies away with it.

To see a cowbird lay her egg you must get up early in the morning. Like the milkman, she comes at dawn. She will approach the nest, stop and look around carefully, climb into the other bird's nest and quickly dispatch her duties with a take it or leave it attitude.

Cowbirds have parasitized more than a hundred species of birds. Usually the smaller birds among their victims disregard the fact that there is an egg in the nest twice as large as its companions. And who could blame a tiny warbler or sparrow for feeling a twinge of pride and inner accomplishment that she should mother such a magnificent egg?

There is usually only one cowbird's egg to the nest. Sometimes a female cowbird may even remove the egg of another cowbird to make room for her own, but she is not always so uncharitable. In 1949, George W. Byers, of the University of Michigan, found a black-and-white warbler's nest with two warbler eggs and eight cowbird eggs. The neighborhood must have been full of optimistic cowbirds. The tiny warbler sat atop the pile of eggs trying in vain to warm them. And after almost twice the usual incubation period, the warbler, frustrated, one may assume, abandoned the nest. She was luckier than she knew. It is about all a pair of warblers or sparrows can manage to feed one ravenous young cowbird. Eight in the same nest would have been a nightmare come true.

A cowbird's egg hatches in eleven to twelve days, usually about the same time or a little before those of the host. But the cowbird has a head start in size and hogs the food supply. He grows fast and crowds the nest. Within a few days this visitor who came uninvited and stayed to dinner is usually the sole survivor.

The carefree life of the cowbird has long excited the interest, perhaps even a twinge of envy, of students of birdlife. They've gone to some lengths to uncover the secrets of the cowbird's success. Some years back T. C. Stephens found, on the shore of Lake Okoboji, Iowa, the nest of a red-eyed vireo with three eggs. One of them was that of a cowbird.

It was an ideal arrangement for close observation. The nest was suspended on a low branch of a red elm. Stephens could stand and look into the nest. He tied a string to the limb and fastened it down a few inches lower. Now he could sit on a camp stool and look into the nest.

And that's what he did for two and a half days. The first day he was there at four forty-five A.M., and he stayed until eight twenty-two in the evening. The three eggs hatched. Within the hour he had inched the stool to within touching distance of the nest, which was essential to his plan.

He stained one of the vireos with methylene blue and named him "Blue." The other one he named "White." The third bird was called, fittingly enough, "Cowbird." The two adult vireos came and went with food so often that Stephens was nearly dizzy with watching them. That day they made 107 trips carrying bugs and worms and snails. (The female did seventy-five percent of the work.)

The ever-hungry cowbird was given fifty-eight percent of the food. Stephens, in scientific fashion, wanted to know what the vireos were offering in this continual lunch. His plan for finding out was simplicity itself. He carried a pair of forceps with which he swiped an occasional snail or spider from the parent birds' beaks.

His notes in one place relate that, "At visit No. 267 the female brought another *Succinea avara*, and I made a determined effort to secure it with my forceps, but failed, and it was fed to White." One can hardly blame the vireo for drawing the line at feeding a fourth fledgling—and this one big enough to cover a camp stool.

The vireos worked fast. Let a fledgling hesitate, and they offered his food to another. One tidbit brought to White would go only halfway down. His parent pulled the food from his beak and promptly

fed it to Cowbird. The adult paid little heed to the
fact that as she pulled the insect from White, she
pulled White right out of the nest and he toppled
to the ground.

The truly scientific approach to this tragedy
would have been to ignore it and record what happened next at the nest. But at this point, humanity
triumphed over science. Stephens, perhaps shaken
by the events of the day, tenderly picked up White
and returned him to the nest. A few days later
Cowbird "mysteriously" disappeared and the young
vireos, unlike most such victims, survived.

Young cowbirds usually leave the nest within ten
days after hatching. But for several more days, until
they're strong enough to fly, they loaf about the
neighborhood while their foster parents work more
furiously than ever to meet the endless demands of
a freeloader twice their size.

Who can be certain? Perhaps the foster parents feel some sentimental attachment toward this
strange-looking fledgling. But he apparently bears
them no love. When he's strong enough to fly, he
abruptly departs from his boardinghouse without
even a "thank you." He ignores the warblers or
sparrows who reared him and promptly adopts the
carefree life of fellow cowbirds cavorting in the
pastures.

Cowbirds apologize to no one for their antisocial
habits. They show no signs of remorse or intentions
of changing their way of living. For centuries on

end their grand scheme has served them well. It is even suspected that, in the world of birds, cowbirds, which seldom fight with others or among themselves, make good neighbors most of the year.

But then comes that inevitable spring morning when the female cowbird follows the example set her by her own parents. Once again with her light-hearted approach to motherhood she bestows her eggs upon her unsuspecting neighbors. It is hard to trust a bird like that.

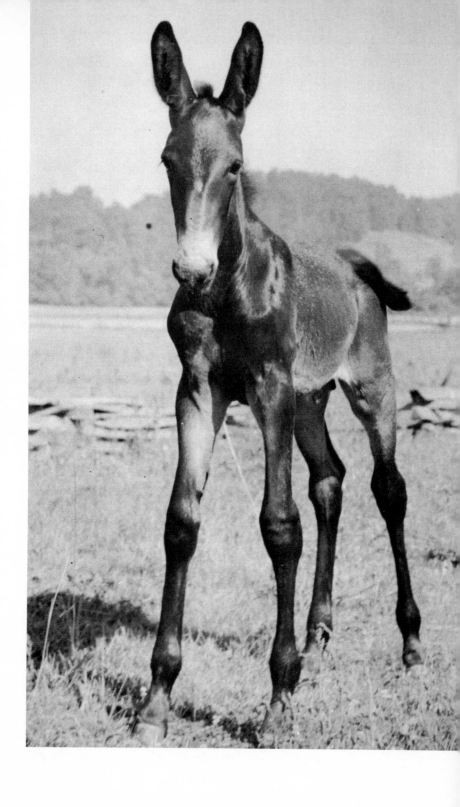

TWO

# *Consider the Mule*

Old-timers get sentimental about many things that have passed from the farm scene, but you seldom hear them weep for the mule.

Love him or not, the mule helped build the country and we owe him much. Hot weather or cold, he has been in there pulling. He withstands the elements better than the horse, eats less hay, pulls more steadily (once he gets started), and generally stays healthier.

When mules were at their peak in this country, there was one bred for every task. Some were sugar mules, tobacco mules, or cotton mules; there were logging mules, potato mules, wagon mules, and mining mules. There were even the mules that inherited the glamorous job of carrying tourists down the cliffside paths of Grand Canyon.

Since the 1920's, gracefully and without protest, the mule has been turning over to the tractor his place in the furrow. By nature he has few cares. Some call him stubborn, while others claim he is only independent. At any rate, he always wanted to be his own master—and generally was.

He holds himself aloof and claims few friends. Unlike the collie dog, he has never learned to wag his tail in pleasure. He lacks the warmth of the horse and the soft look of the cow. Some Missourians say that when your mule kicks you, he is only expressing affection.

Some mules, maybe all of them, carry a streak of pure "orneriness." My father, who as a youth drove long teams of mules through Kansas wheat fields, tells of the mule that once reached down and bit the ear of the man who was feeding him. The mule skinner pulled the mule's ear down and bit deeply into it. "There, you devil," he said, "now you know how it feels." Some people understand mules.

An impulsive mule can be the best thing that ever happened to a quiet community. The best-known mule where I grew up was a big dark beast named "Pete," who had been taken off the farm and put to pulling coal cars. The memory of the warm barn and the alfalfa hay only a half mile down the road was strong in Pete.

About once a week he would run away from the coal mine and race down the road toward the barn at full speed, pulling behind him an empty coal car that banged and swayed dangerously from one side of the road to the other.

We could hear him coming before he even rounded the curve up the road. From the field, house, or barn we would run as near the edge of the road as we dared to see old Pete race past, his neck stretching out and his long legs covering ground faster, it seemed, than any race horse.

My father, in a futile gesture of friendship toward Pete's owner, would run toward the road shouting, "Whoa, Pete, whoa!" But Pete had a downgrade favoring him now. He could feel the wind in his face and his spirits were high. He paid no heed to man nor beast, for visions of alfalfa danced in his head.

Before Pete was out of sight an old coal truck would come down the road, urged to top speed by one intense neighbor bent over the wheel like Barney Oldfield. Beside him sat his brother-in-law, co-owner of the mine, with the door open and one foot on the running board always ready to jump out and capture Pete—or save his own neck. I think, however, he was plain scared, because in all the times Pete ran away we never knew them to catch him short of the barn.

They would bribe him with an armload of alfalfa hay to get the coal car pulled back up the road. Pete had won his point, and when he marched back to the mine he held his head up proudly. A mule is hard to shame.

Even the fact that he's not quite normal in the world of beasts seems to cause him no regrets. His mixed ancestry, a mare and a jack, leaves little room for pride of family line, and the fact that he's sterile robs him of hope for the future. He is his own animal, the beginning and the end.

Man will never know the true depth of the mule's intellect, but many who have worked closely with the beasts are convinced that their hybrid vigor grants them superior intelligence. It was George Washington Carver who observed that, "I never saw a mule that didn't look like he thought he was thinking." Mules, it is said by their admirers, have enough horse sense to give lessons to horses.

Many towns bear the names of animals that loomed large in their history. Oklahoma has its Elk City, New York its Buffalo, and Texas its Muleshoe. Muleshoe, which bears proudly its historic connection with the hybrid beast of burden, borrowed the name years ago from a local cattle brand shaped like a mule's shoe.

As the population grew and the town had its own post office, parking meters, P.T.A., and civic pride, it did not forsake the mule. In recent times, after the Agricultural Census revealed a steadily dwindling mule population throughout America, Muleshoe citizens doubled and redoubled their efforts to preserve the memory of the animal. The local radio station's call letters became KMUL. Civic leaders formed the Mule Memorial Association. The major purpose of the Association was to raise money for a life-sized fiberglass statue of a mule. Money came from many parts of the world, and the statue stands today where U. S. Highways 70 and 84 intersect, squarely in the middle of Muleshoe.

Much of the mule's fame stems from his hind feet. As a kicker his aim is accurate and his strength great. Some say imaginative mules can even kick forward like a cow.

At the height of her glory as the top producer of fine mules, the state of Missouri advertised widely with a picture of a farmer leading a pair of mules. Below it was printed, "In mules—Missouri stands in the lead—the only safe place."

An honest mule would not argue the point.

# THREE

# *Barnyard Extrovert*

Goats have lived with people for thousands of years, but people are still impressed with goats more than goats are impressed by people. All man's efforts have failed to change the goat or curb his spirits. He's as independent today as ever.

One of our neighbors who kept milk goats for more than twenty years is still amazed at what they can figure out for themselves. There was a time when his granary door could be opened only by reaching through a slot and pulling a rope inside. Surely this granary should be safe from goats. That's what the neighbor thought until he began finding the door open each time he went to the barn.

Finally, hiding behind a cider barrel, he saw one of his older nanny goats pitty-pat up to the granary door, stand on her rear feet, stick her head through the slot, and jerk on the ring until the door swung wide. "A goat that smart," my neighbor said, "deserves a little extra grain," and he let her eat her fill before he chased her out and equipped the door with a goat-proof latch.

Nature has equipped this animal admirably to cope with all manner of difficult obstacles. He can clamber, crawl, climb and jump over automobiles, hay stacks, tractors and combines. Fences are a delightful challenge to him, and about the lowest fence expected to hold him is a five-footer topped by a strand of barbed wire.

Goats sometimes develop a scientific approach to electric fences; they learn how to test them each morning. If the current is on and the ground is wet enough, they leave the fence alone—until the next day—then test it again. Many a thirsty goat has learned to turn the water faucet on. The trouble is he seldom bothers to turn it off again.

A goat keeps up a restless search for excitement. He may climb to the top of a shiny new automobile and slide down the windshield. He hungers for linens hanging on the line. Flowers and shrubs delight him as something to eat rather than to look at. Porch furniture and rocking chairs are playthings. He leaps into them, rocks off, and goes back for more.

Goat lovers hate to see them vilified, as they have been through the ages. Even before Geoffrey Chaucer wrote, six hundred years ago, his famous line, "He stinken as a goat," everyone thought goats stinken. Truth is that only the bucks at mating season carry a strong odor. There is an old superstition that the spirit of the devil is lodged in the goat. And there's an old Persian proverb, "If you think you have trouble, buy a goat." To those who really know goats, however, such prejudices are unfounded. Further, never tell a goat raiser that goats eat tin cans. The labels, yes, and the contents if they can get them, but the cans—impossible.

Believe him, however, when he tells you of some other strange things goats will eat. Goats have the toughest mouths of all ruminants. They chew, swallow and obviously enjoy briars. Nettles tickle them. They clean up weeds and brambles more refined livestock will ignore. This is why they make such good companions for cows or sheep on brushy hillsides.

And of all the strange foods goats like, poison ivy is a favorite. What's poison to some is salad to the goat. When the poison ivy is gone, a goat will eat pasture and hay. A ton of hay plus pasture (the rougher the better) will keep three goats a year.

The four most popular registered breeds of milk goats in this country are Toggenburg, an easy-going brown goat said to come originally from Switzerland; the popular Nubian with his long drooping

ears; the white-haired Saanen; and the French
Alpine.

The American Milk Goat Registry Association has
some fourteen hundred members scattered across
the country. One goat expert estimates that perhaps
ten thousand Americans keep milk goats. Some
herds, especially in California, have as many as
five hundred goats on the milking line. Big herds
are often machine-milked. Each day a good goat can
yield a gallon of milk worth forty to seventy cents
a quart. Goat milk comes already homogenized and
is widely acclaimed as a health food.

I once knew a goat-dairy owner who walked
home behind his herd of milk goats from the far end
of his farm every evening. One of his neighbors re-
marked that it made a pretty sight, the farmer driv-
ing his goats home at eventide. "M'am," he said, "I
don't drive goats. Nobody drives goats. I'm just
leading them from behind."

Goats deserve to carry themselves proudly. What
other barnyard animal combines so adeptly a love
of life, liberty and the pursuit of happiness with
noble history and indomitable spirit?

But this same spirit will keep goats in trouble as
long as people and goats associate. Recently I read
in our local weekly newspaper about the trial of a
man who swore to sit in jail forever before he would
live with a goat again.

The judge listened carefully while this goat hater
told of shooting his wife's pet goat in the living

room. (He was charged as well with pointing the gun at his wife.) The goat was only three weeks old. But three weeks, the defendant insisted, just before being released for insufficient evidence, is too long to live with any goat.

It's as we said in the beginning, you either like goats or you don't. And whichever it is, it could not matter less to this barnyard extrovert.

FOUR

# *The Famous Hopper*

Look closely at the next grasshopper you encounter. Within that strangely shaped little body lie amazing talents. Consider, for example, how skillfully the grasshopper can hop. Those who measure such things assure us that a grasshopper can leap ten times as high as the length of his body, or do a broad jump twenty times the length of his body, using only his legs and not his wings. A human being thus endowed could jump to the top of the silo or leap over the barn.

If he chooses to call to other grasshoppers, he does not sing but fiddles instead. Some species of grasshoppers call by rubbing their wings together and others by rubbing their wings against parts of

GRASSHOPPER

the hind legs. As if jumping and fiddling were not enough for grasshoppers to ask of their unusual legs, some even hear with them because their ears are behind their knee joints.

Sunshine seems to be made for grasshoppers. Most of them hide at night, out of sight and out of reach. But in daytime throughout the summer they leap through the meadows, jumping gaily over daisies and bull thistles as though grasshoppers haven't a care in the world.

But don't you believe it. They have plenty of troubles. That is one reason they hop so much. Often they are only one jump ahead of tragedy. Even if we disregard the everlasting war waged on them by people, grasshoppers must still beware of rodents, birds, spiders, reptiles, fungus and bacteria.

And if they only knew it they would treat a certain tiny, freeloading wasp as another of their enemies. Grasshoppers do not realize that there are little parasitic wasps that lay their eggs with grasshopper eggs. Nor do they know that the larvae of these wasps will eat the young of the grasshopper. How does the female wasp locate the eggs which the grasshopper takes the precaution of burying in the soil? To search at random for them would be hopeless; she might never find a home for her little wasps that way. But she simplifies the process by attaching herself to the female grasshopper and is on the scene when the grasshopper eggs are cached in the earth.

Now the little hitchhiker gets off and waits. The

female grasshopper carries a drilling tool on the end of her ovipositor with which she bores a hole in the ground. Then, depending on which species of grasshopper she represents, she tenderly places anywhere from twenty-five to one hundred and twenty-five eggs in the tiny cavern. Now she covers them with a fluid which hardens to form an egg case or "pod."

But if her little parasitic traveling companion has been standing there in her shadow, there are now wasp eggs dropped among the grasshopper eggs. Only wasps are likely to come up where grasshoppers were planted.

There are some six hundred species of grasshoppers known in the United States. They are divided into two families, the long-horned and the short-horned. Those known as locusts have shorter antennae than do the common meadow grasshoppers. The short-horned grasshoppers are the locusts that darkened the skies and laid bare the land in Biblical times and in modern times as well.

On one such occasion, as related in Exodus, it was not until the Lord sent a strong west wind that the insects were swept from the land to their destruction in the Red Sea. The modern campaign against the grasshopper really reaches back to 1874. That year grasshoppers crossed the Great Plains in clouds. They shaded the earth from the sun. Agriculture was stricken; businesses faltered. Government economists computed that grasshoppers ate 200 million dollars worth of crops in two years. In 1876 Congress appropriated 18,000 dollars to establish an entomological commission. Three specialists were assigned to study the grasshopper and report on what could be done to shortstop these insects.

Before long the new commission uncovered details on how deep the grasshoppers place their eggs and what kind of fields they choose for them. Consequently, farmers, following the newest advice, began plowing deep and destroying the eggs. Most destructive grasshoppers lay their eggs in the late summer or early autumn, and the young do not hatch until the following spring.

Next, researchers developed a plan for feeding grasshoppers bran that was treated with arsenic. This new dietary supplement was introduced to the world of grasshoppers in 1885. Large scale spreading of these grasshopper baits continued until 1948, when more potent insecticides were introduced. That year insecticides were first spread by airplane in the war on grasshoppers. The next year 500 airplanes flying at altitudes of about 150 feet blitzed the grasshoppers. Today entire regions can be quickly treated against grasshopper damage from airplanes or trucks spreading sprays or mists of such potent chemical insecticides as aldrin or malathion. It is doubtful that grasshoppers will ever again rise to the peaks of abundance they knew in ancient times or in the Great Plains of North America in the last century.

Even so, hardly a year passes that hordes of grasshoppers do not visit destruction on some agricultural area in some part of the United States. Whether they are eating away at wheat on the prairielands, cotton in the South, vegetables in New England, or corn in the Midwest, they cannot be long ignored by men who work the land.

But if all the grasshoppers were gone from the earth, who would feed the sparrow hawk, the Franklin's gull and the parasitic wasp? And what would gleeful country children chase and sometimes catch without having anybody care?

# FIVE

# The Shepherd's Best Friend

In all of dogdom there may be no more amazing animal than the sharp-witted little border collie. His love of work alone is enough to set him apart. While other dogs fritter their time away chasing rabbits or sleeping in the shade, their cousin, the border collie, is out there hard at work and loving every minute of it.

The reason for this trait reaches back hundreds of years and into the border country between England and Scotland. Shepherds there have always selected their dogs for brains and "git up." Modern border collies are still chosen that way. Color, coat, and conformity are left for the bench show breeds. All

BORDER COLLIE

the border-collie man asks of his dog is that old-fashioned love of work.

Here is a dog with race-horse speed on the short dash, and an alertness that tells him which way a sheep will move almost before the sheep himself knows. What's more he is so devoted to his master that as one owner said, "I think he would jump into fire if I asked him to."

Little wonder that half the border collies sold now go for pets, and that breeders seldom have enough pups to fill their orders.

Shepherds tell endless tales which demonstrate how the intelligence of the border collie has paid off. In Wooster, Ohio, Carl Bradford, one of the country's leading breeders of working border collies, one evening sent one of his dogs to bring in the flock. The dog drove the flock past an old platform. But as soon as he had them headed for the barn, the dog turned and went back to the platform. And he stayed there until Bradford went out and found a sheep hopelessly stuck beneath the boards. "The dog knew," says Bradford, "that he wasn't supposed to come in without all of them."

One shepherd, disturbed when the sheep came in without the dog, found his dog far back in the fields lying beside a newborn lamb, waiting for help.

Bradford's interest in the border collies goes back more than a quarter of a century, when he saw some of the dogs worked in an eastern state. "I thought," he recalls, "that it must take a genius to work dogs like that." He has since altered that opinion. "Anyone who wants to work these dogs and sticks with it can do it," he says. "You don't have to know more than the dogs." The steady search for better dogs has sent Bradford and his two sons to Scotland and England to select native working border collies to bring them back to Wooster. He has worked his outstanding dogs at numerous shows and exhibitions.

Most American shepherds speak a brand of English these dogs from the heather cannot understand. So rather than confuse their new dogs with new American words the Bradfords adopted the pronunciations of British and Scotch shepherds. Where is the American-born working dog that would understand that "la doon" really means "lie down," or that "quay-ta-me" means "go away to me"?

The good border collie will put a flock of sheep wherever his master wants them or hold them wherever he asks. He will "tather" from either left or right. He moves in slowly behind the flock until they begin to gather and move away from him.

He can hold the sheep from a prone position. He casts a roving eye on his flock, constantly alert to the slightest change. And he creeps forward eyeing his flock as he goes, moving one foot at a time. Should the master want to catch an individual sheep, two of these dogs can bring the herd close enough to make them stumble over the shepherd. Meanwhile the shepherd can ignore his dogs. They will handle their part of the task if he takes care of his.

One owner even uses his border collie to unload steers from railroad cars, a ticklish and highly dangerous job for any dog. The steers packed into a tight space seldom appreciate having a dog nip their heels. Their hoofs rattle the sides of the enclosure. Where is the dog in this melee of flying hoofs? He's flat on his belly, creeping from one animal to the next, here a nip, there a nip. The frustrated steers clear the area without touching him.

Some border collies will even get up and run lightly across the backs of the sheep to get them moving from the front, and then come back by the same bridge.

Bradford once had a stubborn ram that tried twice to pin a dog against the inside of a chute. Twice the dog jumped the fence to escape. The third time, however, the dog grabbed the surprised ram by the leg, and this time the ram jumped the fence.

But the border collie never forgot nor forgave. The same ram, accustomed to trailing the flock, was always the sheep the dog picked on when told to speed up his flock. When the ram began traveling in the middle of the flock, the collie would cut into it to get at him. Sheep have to learn that the border collie is boss. The dog has always known it.

SIX

# *The Antique Cattle*

Styles in cattle, like styles in bathing suits and tractors, change. And just as some people like to see early threshing machines and old automobiles, others like to see antique cattle. The oldest of this country's cattle, and perhaps the most famous, are the Texas longhorns, fabled lean creatures, evil of temper and tough of sinew. There are still a few left and you can even buy one.

Citizens who trace their history to the Mayflower and beyond are newcomers to this land compared to the longhorns. As far back as 1521 Gregorio de Villalobos brought a shipment of these old Spanish cattle from Santo Domingo. Then along came

HORNS

Coronado and others with still more of the rangy cattle from Mexico. These animals became the foundation of the cattle industry in all of the Southwest. They were a type, more than a separate breed. And a modern beefman, just looking at a longhorn, shakes his head and wonders where the hamburger comes from.

Here was an animal that could withstand the thousand-mile march, cold, heat, and thirst of the Chisholm Trail. Between 1866 and 1890 more than ten million longhorns, vast herds of cantankerous, milling cattle, were driven up from Texas northward toward the rail centers. This was the time and the longhorn was the animal that made the American cowboy the hero of children in many lands.

Then the railroads pushed farther into the plains country and over the western mountains. The rumbling cars hauled out the cattle whose ancestors had walked to market. Ranchers began bringing in English type bulls to mix with the longhorn blood. Soon the longhorns were almost totally replaced by shorter, stockier cattle that produced more meat from the range grasses. The longhorns were going, and no one seemed to care.

But when the curtain was almost down on the old-fashioned steer with his magnificent horns, a couple of forest rangers at the Wichita National Forest and Game Preserve in Commanche County, Oklahoma, decided to save some of the cattle as a living historic exhibit. Congress appropriated money for the project.

Eventually, after checking 30,000 head of cattle they put together a herd of 27 genuine longhorns, last survivors of a colorful cattle industry. The longhorns were brought to Wichita Mountains, and there they have been left to run almost wild in a great enclosed refuge that covers many miles of that rocky rangeland. This is the biggest remaining herd of Texas longhorns, and the herd is held at about 300 animals. Every year the surplus is sold at public auction.

Those horns that brought the longhorn fame had little value to the animal that carried them. True, with the tip of his horn, he could scratch an itch he might otherwise never reach. But the fact that his horns made shiny impressive trophies on many a rathskeller wall probably never did impress the longhorn favorably. His horns, in fact, could damage beef on those long drives when the animals were pushed together at a river's edge or in some narrow passage.

The steers in the herd carry the truly impressive horns. Many of them measure five feet from tip to tip, and there is a record of one set reaching more than eight feet across. Cows, on the other hand, often have twisting horns. But the bulls, alas, even though they are kings of their tribes, are endowed with puny horns which should make them envious of their impotent offspring.

The longhorns carry more variety in colors than a stack of feed sacks. The longhorns' colors are not brilliant but they are varied hues and patterns of blues, reds, browns, and whites. There are the roans, speckled, pied, and brindles. Those who manage today's remaining longhorn herds breed the cattle to match the hues of the animals that walked the old trails.

The longhorn had his beginning in a day when type was not too important. But if you suddenly found yourself judging longhorns at the county fair you might remember the standards established by the managers of Wichita Mountains National Wildlife Refuge. The longhorn, you would be told, is fairly large boned, rangy, and short coupled. They have long faces with wide-set eyes. Cows should average 650 to 750 pounds, and steers of four or five years should weigh half-a-ton. There have been steers weighing more than 2,000 pounds.

It is difficult sometimes to tell what a longhorn steer is thinking as he stands staring at you. If he moves toward you, however, you may assume that he is not coming up to be petted. Consider his superior weight and speed and the pair of weapons mounted on his head. Climb a tree, get under an automobile, or vacate the premises.

The history of the West's cattle industry has been dominated by the longhorn. He is a lean animal with a hungry look, long on horn, short on beef, not a thing of beauty, but as practical in his day as the grain cradle and the ox yoke, all of them now relegated to the dimming past.

# SEVEN

# *Pigeon Talk*

Pigeons should teach chickens a thing or two. Consider drinking, for example. The chicken is an old-fashioned drinker. He has to lift his head every time he gets a beakful of water to let the liquid trickle down his throat. But the talented pigeon sucks water up as if through a drinking straw.

Pigeons are respected for other accomplishments too. They know how to navigate. Even when they do not know where they are, they know how to find their way home. For thousands of years people have wondered how pigeons do this. This would be a handy thing for people to know, but pigeons are secretive about the whole business. They don't, how-

ever, seem to mind helping people out once in a
while.

History books leave no record of the first man to
use pigeons to carry messages. But military leaders
have used pigeons as messengers for centuries.
When Caesar conquered Gaul, he wanted the home-
town folks back in Rome to know about it right
away. Whom did he send? A pigeon, of course.

When Napoleon ran into serious trouble at Water-
loo, the sad news was carried home by pigeons.

The talented pigeon is still getting new jobs because of his homing ability. One medical center near
Washington, D. C., sends its doctors out on house
calls carrying pigeons in their little black bags along
with stethoscopes. If the doctor needs a fast diag-
nosis of a body fluid, he attaches a one-ounce vial
to the harness of a pigeon and turns the bird loose.
The bird flies straight to the roof of the medical center. Laboratory technicians make a fast analysis and
telephone the results to the waiting doctor. In this
age of crowded traffic the pigeon gets through faster
than an automobile courier, especially during rush
hours.

Or consider the delivery service pigeons perform
for farm people in far off Formosa. Cattle semen is
flown to Formosa from a breeder's co-op in Wisconsin. But in Formosa it is shortstopped by im-
passable mountain roads. Pigeons, however, deliver
the semen promptly to technicians in the remote
farming settlements.

There are some 289 species of doves or pigeons around the world. They carry a strong family resemblance, having stout bodies, short necks, small heads, and short beaks. They all have a gentle cooing or booming voice. The sounds they make are pleasant the first few times. But pigeons don't know when to stop cooing, and the monotony of their call sometimes diminishes their popularity. They are vegetarians by nature. Grains, seed, and fruit please them. They seem also to need salt regularly.

The common pigeon of barnyard and city street traces his family line to the rock dove of Europe and Asia. Men have selected them for various traits until there are some two hundred varieties. But turn domesticated pigeons back to the wild, and within a few generations their descendants resemble again the age-old rock doves.

They have lived in close association with men now for more than five thousand years. Many societies have considered them religious symbols. Perhaps people like them because they seem to be gentle creatures of peace and good will. They are pictured carrying olive branches, and they are turned loose over the international games at the World Olympics. Respected as they are by poets, philosophers, and young lovers it is shocking to learn that they fight among themselves. The pigeon that invades another's nesting territory should go prepared for battle.

Pigeons may not be perfect, but at least they are

not fickle. They mate for life. Having reached such agreements they are likely to set up housekeeping among the rafters of the barn. There on a ledge, they make what a pigeon thinks is a nest. People and Baltimore orioles think it is a simple platform of small sticks loosely assembled. Here the female tenderly deposits her two white-shelled treasures.

The parents take turns incubating the eggs, usually the female at night and the male by day. This goes on for seventeen days. The two young birds, raised on regurgitated "pigeon milk," are ready to leave the nest in two or three weeks. More than likely, however, the mother bird has already started her next family nearby. Domestic pigeons will sometimes raise twelve squabs a year.

Men are still figuring out new and complicated jobs for pigeons. Pigeons have been trained to inspect pills and recognize those of imperfect shape and color, and then to peck a device that removes them from the production line. Psychologists have taught them this by rewarding them with food each time they recognize a bad pill. This seems quite an accomplishment for both scientists and pigeons.

# EIGHT

# Crawfish Have Their Troubles

It is time that the crawfish be brought up from his little wet world for a closer look. People have taken him for granted for far too long. Of course he is ugly, except perhaps to another crawfish, but he is too interesting, complex, valuable and tasty to deserve obscurity.

It is not as if the crawfish cares. He would as soon men left him to his own devices. But the crawfish is relished by such a long list of predators, man included, that it is little wonder he has developed through the eons one of the speediest reverse gears of any shallow-water creature. He spends most of his life backing away from trouble, and he makes no excuse for leaving the scene of an accident that is about to happen to him.

Wild creatures from rock bass to kingfishers find crawfish irresistible. Bass, bullheads, bluegills, and bullfrogs relish them. Raccoons, herons and practically anything else that can catch them will eat them. Life in the crawdad hole is one continual game of catch. Even crawfish eat crawfish. They can trust no one.

The two-hundred-odd species of crawfish in the United States look much alike and resemble nothing else except lobsters and shrimp. Out in front of its pointed little head each has a pair of fearsome looking pincers lined with sharp serrations which make for a better grip on items of food or human fingers. It wears its skeleton on the outside like a coat of armor.

Crawfish range in size from one to sixteen inches. The biggest one I ever saw was brought aboard a fishing boat in the Caribbean some years ago. The captain, a suntanned little man whose whole life had been spent working around harbors and bays knew a good thing when he tasted it. He spotted a commercial fishing boat off to the east and toward evening dispatched our small boat over to bargain with the fishermen for crawfish for supper. They came back with a water bucket full of them.

One of the crawfish was half again as big as the rest, and at first sight of this fine looking crustacean the captain grabbed him and happily held him up for all to see. On board was a photographer who immediately wanted a portrait of the big crawfish. While the captain held it aloft, the crawfish suddenly flipped its powerful tail, banged down on the deck, and immediately went into reverse. It was going with uncanny speed toward the edge of the deck and the open sea. The captain, aware that his prize was escaping, bounded over the deck and made an ungraceful grab for the crustacean just as it dropped over the edge and splashed into the sea. The crawfish settled on the bottom and stared up through twelve feet of wonderfully clear salt water at a boat captain who seemed near tears. It was a tragedy—except perhaps for the crawfish.

If in spring or summer you should visit that part of Louisiana where the Mississippi meanders lazily through the low country, you'll find people who really appreciate the crawfish. For more than two centuries Louisiana people have known the crawfish as a delicacy. Perhaps no place else in the world are crawfish eaten in such numbers. But the fun, they'll tell you, is half in the eating and half in the catching.

When crawfishing hits its peak, the populace sets out with crawfish nets, baskets and gunny sacks. People slop through flooded lowlands or visit the nearest cypress swamps. Men, women, children, teachers, farmers, and businessmen, all engage in earnest pursuit of the "mudbug."

Meanwhile Louisiana's commercial fishermen

each year capture about 1,200,000 pounds of crawfish for restaurants and consumers who cannot catch
their own.

There has been a note of sadness settling over this
crawfish country in recent times. All is not well.
Crawfish populations have fallen at a rate that dis-
turbs both commercial and sport fishermen. Biologists credit the drop to a combination of changing
water levels, low food supply, and increased feeding
by fish. The search for a solution has resulted in the
establishment of one of the world's most unusual
farms.

As crawfish became more scarce, the hue and
cry was heard all the way to the state legislature.
Spurred on by the crawfish fanciers, the legislators
quickly appropriated 10,000 dollars. This was to en-
able the state Wild Life and Fisheries Commission
to build the world's first crawfish research farm.

Events moved rapidly. A Fisheries Commission
biologist designed the farm and it was soon under
construction at Cecelia. A few months later crawfish
enthusiasts journeyed to Cecelia for the dedication
ceremonies. The high point in the day came when
a state representative solemnly poured onto the new
farm a Mason jarful of water from a nearby crawfish
hole.

Some crawfish live not in stream or lake but in wet
meadows. If you hear a farmer say he has crawfish
land—that's just what he has: tight clay soil, usually,
riddled with crawfish burrows. Their dwellings are

marked by chimneys of soil which the crawfish have piled up, sometimes a foot-and-a-half high. The burrows themselves may go three feet deep and end in a pocket which the crawfish hollows out for a living room.

One species of crawfish that inhabits 1,000 square miles of Alabama and Mississippi farmland does its best to even the score with man. These crawfish which have learned the art of fasting go without food for as long as nine months at a time. Then, when it is summertime and the cotton is high, they bestir themselves just long enough to come up out of the ground and consume all the succulent greenery in sight. This is the signal for the farmer to force creosote into the crawfish holes. But he does it with a sigh of resignation because as surely as spring comes again the crawfish will be back.

Among the strangest of all crawfish are the blind ones that dwell in caves. Mammoth cave has blind, white crawfish that have lived for eons in total darkness.

Crawfish are not lovable. They fight with each other at the drop of a feeler, do battle with a vengeance and likely lose a leg or two in the fray. But the loss of a leg is seldom tragic. The part cut off continues to grow, for crawfish have the power of regeneration. Even if one loses an eye, the eye can grow back.

Life for a crawfish starts in March or June when the female lays her eggs. If you have collected crawfish at this season you may have seen the females carrying eggs. They keep their treasure with them constantly. The eggs, as they come from the female's body, are handed back to the underside of her tail with little appendages called swimmerets.

During the next three weeks the eggs, perhaps a hundred of them, are carried around attached to the female by an adhesive. They are aerated as she fans them constantly with her tail. The newborn crawfish do not leave home immediately. They stay with their mother, attached to the shells of their eggs, tiny, inactive crawfish feeding on microscopic life and growing rapidly. They go through their first molt within two days and within a week they molt a second time. By this time they crawl in brief exploratory trips over the mother's body and scamper back to safety beneath her tail at the first sign of danger.

If you are curious about the age of a freshwater crawfish, there is a rule of thumb for estimating it in the fall. Measure the crawfish in inches and subtract one to get its approximate age in years. The vast majority of crawfish do not live past their second year and a four-year-old is an ancient member of the crawfish clan.

Molting of the shell is highly important in the life of a crawfish. The reason is simple. His body grows but his shell does not. Sooner or later his suit of armor is too tight and it has to come off. Meanwhile, a new pliable shell forms beneath the old one. For a time the crawfish wears two suits.

This is the time when bait dealers and anglers know him as a "peeler." With a little practice you can pick out the peelers. The body and tail are darker in color. And if you apply pressure gently with thumb and forefinger to the sides of the tail, the shell gives a little. The shell of a peeler dents easily behind the head. Within a day or so, if everything is favorable, these peelers will shed and become soft craws.

This is a big day for any crawfish. The process is slow, laborious and filled with hazard. When he goes into his peeler stage, he lies in shallow water with his back sticking above the surface for about two days. The shell dries out and internal pressure begins to split it open.

Now the creature takes cover beneath some rock or other shelter. He begins a series of contortions that rip an opening in the shell almost the length of the back. After this, he lies on his back squirming and fighting to free himself from his old shell. His soft body buckles and bends. Part by part he escapes the shell which he has outgrown.

But there is still much tedious work for him. The legs must be pulled from the old shell for their full length, and the soft parts can break easily. There are ten of these legs to work free and ten tiny mouthparts.

Then there are the claws, and they are much larger than the tiny hollow joints through which the crawfish must pull them to free them from the old shell. As though this were not enough to ask of a crawfish, he must also shed the lining from his digestive tract, an act that calls for intestinal fortitude.

For an hour after this ordeal he lies helpless beside his cast-off armor. Right after he molts and until calcium works back into his shell, he is a soft craw. Everything that swims, crawls or walks is out to consume him, and no matter how well he hides or how fast he backs away from trouble his future down there among the rocks is seldom secure.

We are assured by a professor of zoology that, "The best time to collect soft craws for fish bait is early morning." The peelers have shed during the night. A better plan yet is to collect the peelers the day before they shed. Put them into a shallow tank. Then after they shed, put them in moss. Because they should be kept in a cool place, slip them into the bottom shelf of the refrigerator. They will be too cold to crawl around much and the moss, plus refrigeration, slows down the hardening process. This way you may have paper-shelled craws for a week or ten days.

# NINE

# *The Untidy Ones*

Although it has been three decades since my friend Karl Maslowski rode in a rumble seat with a turkey vulture, he remembers it, "as though it were yesterday. The rumble seat," he says, "was made for love, but that turkey vulture and I weren't very compatible."

Karl, widely known for his nature movies, began his career as a professional naturalist early in life. Consequently, when a farmer on the other side of Clermont County sent word that he had located the nest of a turkey vulture in his wood lot, Karl felt compelled to view the nest close up. He called a friend who was one of the few young people in the neighborhood to own a car in those depression days.

As soon as Karl saw the ungainly vulture squatting over her two speckled white eggs, he decided to take her back to town and band her. "If you're going to take that bird back," announced his friend, who knew a little bit about vultures himself, "the two of you will have to ride in the rumble seat."

Anyone experienced with vultures knows that when they are frightened they may regurgitate. Karl's vulture controlled her fear while being captured and settled into the open rear seat of the car. She was contained in a gunny sack with only her naked red head protruding. When the motor started the vulture performed just as predicted. "I found," says Karl, "that I had put the wrong end in the gunny sack."

After he had banded the bird they returned her to the nest, and the old vulture hatched her eggs as though nothing had happened.

Best known of this country's vultures is the turkey vulture which can be found through much of the United States. He has a six-foot wingspread, long, narrow tail, and a naked head which is red in the adults and blackish in the immature birds. Aloft, the turkey vulture carries its wings held above the horizontal.

The black vulture, which is primarily a bird of the southeastern states and was once a common semi-domesticated scavenger in the streets of some southern cities, is smaller than the turkey vulture. His wingspread is less than five feet. When seen from

below his tail looks shorter. His head is black instead of red. He is less skilled at gliding than his red-headed cousin.

Still a third and very rare member of the family found in this country is the California condor. There remain probably no more than a few dozen of these giant birds with their nine-foot wingspread. They live today only in the more remote and rugged sections of the Los Padres National Forest where a sanctuary has been established in hope of saving them from extinction.

Vultures are most appealing at great distances. On the ground they are clumsy and, to many people, repulsive. But once airborne, few animals in all nature are more graceful. Their effortless flight has inspired earthbound men for ages. To this day our best flying efforts make us look like bumblers in an element the buzzards have mastered.

Watch a vulture someday as he climbs higher and higher into the sky. How does he accomplish this feat without ever once flapping his great wings? He does it in summer by riding the warm updrafts. His motionless, outstretched wings catch the warm currents rising from the earth and the air gently lifts him farther and farther above the earth until he is a speck in the sky. Then he may disappear completely from your sight. He will stay aloft for hours on end in fair weather and for long periods won't bother to flap a wing.

But when he is circling low enough for you to

watch him, you can see him move his head occa-
sionally from side to side. While he stays aloft he
spends much of his time cruising in search of food.
To write pleasantly of a "buzzard's" eating habits is
a challenge. These are the carrion eaters. Their diet
is unthinkable, their manners unbearable. But they
spare us many an onerous task, and for it we heap
abuse upon their heads. Vultures and people should
agree that there's no accounting for tastes and let it
go at that.

In a southern state, recently, I was talking with
a dairy farmer who told of a group of black vultures
attacking and killing one of his newborn calves. It
sometimes happens that carrion is scarce and the
black vultures turn to small sheep, pigs, and calves.
They will also, on occasion, destroy small birds in
heron and egret rookeries. But these attacks by vultures on living animals are local affairs and should
not lead to any general warfare against all vultures.
Federal law protects the vulture as a migratory bird.
This law is sound because the vulture is largely a
useful creature.

For more than a century naturalists have engaged
in lengthy arguments about how the vulture finds
his food. Does he see it, or do his nostrils guide him
to it?

John James Audubon tried to settle this question
in 1835. Audubon hid a decaying carcass in a dense
canebrake so that it could not have been easily seen
from above. And it was not. Although vultures

circled the skies overhead none came to dinner.

Audubon then hid carrion beneath a brush shelter, and in this instance also no vultures came around. Still not satisfied, Audubon devised an elaborate test in which he covered carrion with a tarpaulin and on top of that he spread fresh meat. The vultures found the fresh meat but never did look under the canvas.

As the final clincher Audubon tested a blinded vulture. When the bird could not even detect decaying meat held within an inch of its nostrils, one could hardly argue with Audubon's conclusion that a vulture's olfactory senses are unimportant in its search for food. The vulture, it appeared, depended entirely on his eyes to locate his food.

But ornithologist Dr. Frank M. Chapman was at least one scientist not yet convinced. Working with turkey vultures on Barro Colorado Island, Panama, in 1929, Dr. Chapman came up with some different conclusions. The turkey vultures in this case were attracted to the scene repeatedly by completely hidden bait. Turkey vultures, Dr. Chapman concluded, have a "highly developed" sense of smell. His final analysis was that they locate their food by a combination of sight and smell.

More recently Dr. Kenneth E. Stager, ornithologist with the Los Angeles County Museum, brought modern techniques to bear on the question and may have ended the argument Audubon started so many years ago. Dr. Stager, experimenting with turkey vultures in the late 1950's, set up a fan to blow the odors of decaying materials out through chimneys so the birds could not possibly see the source of the food. Vultures upwind ignored the temptations, those downwind wheeled and came looking for the delicacies. Then Dr. Stager placed a mule deer, mounted to look like a carcass, where vultures could see it. They ignored it. But when it was replaced with an actual carcass, vultures soon came in to feed.

Meanwhile, oil company engineers had learned that vultures could help them locate leaks in gas lines. They introduced a foul smelling gas into the lines, then patrolled to see where the vultures assembled. The big birds settled all around the leaking pipes in their search for the source of the attractive odors. All these items considered, there is no longer much doubt that the turkey vulture follows his nose to dinner.

When they locate food they begin to circle the area, and eventually come in at great speed. This is a signal for all other vultures for miles around to gather at the festive board. Researchers are largely convinced that vultures have little or no sense of taste, and perhaps it is just as well.

Aside from his eyesight and his flying, the vulture has no reason to feel superior unless, perhaps, he knows about the fuss made over him once a year in Hinckley Township on the outskirts of Cleveland, Ohio. Never before in history have so many people

paid so much attention to the turkey vulture. This is
the only place known to set aside an annual day
in honor of buzzards. Every year now the citizens
officially designate the first Sunday in spring as
"Buzzard Sunday."

Through much of their range vultures do little if
any migrating. But in northern states where snow
covers their feeding grounds, they have little choice
but to go farther south for the winter months.
Patrolmen for the Cleveland Metropolitan Park System had known for years that the turkey vultures
were regular about their return trips. In fact, one
patrolman, Walter Nawalaniec, had noted for many
years that about seventy-five vultures always came
back on March 15th to roost on Whipp's Ledges
along Hinckley Ridge. It happened so regularly
that Nawalaniec no longer viewed it as unusual.
Capistrano had its swallows; Hinckley had its
"buzzards."

Then a few weeks ahead of the scheduled buzzard return in 1957 the patrolman was talking with
Robert Bordner, a staff member of the *Cleveland
Press* who specializes in local history. Not only had
he been welcoming back the buzzards for several
years, explained Nawalaniec, but the patrolman
before him had also noted that they came on
March 15th. Together they had seen the vultures
return the same day of the year for more than a
quarter of a century.

Bordner predicted in print when the vultures
would return to Hinckley that year. Interest in the

whole affair built up rapidly. The story spilled over into other communities. There were inhabitants of Hinckley who resented the fact that the only thing Hinckley was famous for was a buzzard roost.

Bordner, who, according to park naturalist Harold Wallin, should be given full credit for getting the buzzard celebration started, reported that "Hinckley Township was split down its rural middle, some of the folks resenting identification with such a repulsive, revolting, verminous, stinking, bad mannered eater of carrion."

As the appointed day approached, Wallin had moments of misgiving. The 15th was Friday. The following Sunday was almost certain to bring hundreds of added visitors to the park at Hinckley. People began arriving at dawn. Some came from Pennsylvania and Indiana. Some came prepared to hike and others were dressed in their church clothes. Suddenly it seemed everyone was a bird watcher, or at least a buzzard watcher. There were nine thousand visitors on hand that Sunday to welcome the birds back to their roosts.

All the facilities seemed inadequate. There was a shortage of places for cold visitors to warm themselves, and a shortage of places to eat lunch, while parking facilities and park police were sorely taxed.

By Monday morning the citizens of Hinckley were looking upon the buzzard with new respect.

The next year things were ready for the visiting buzzard watchers. The schoolhouse was opened so people could come in and get warm. Starting at dawn community women organized by the Chamber of Commerce began serving a "Buzzard Breakfast." This turned out to be more appetizing than it sounded; all the hotcakes, sausage and coffee you could consume at one sitting for $1.25 for adults and 75 cents for children. Visitors came and went throughout the day. The crowds were bigger than ever, and people came from farther away. One visitor even came up from Texas.

Within two years Hinckley's Buzzard Sunday crowds, according to a community leader Herman Drews, had grown to 15,000 and it took half-a-ton of pancake flour to serve them.

Hinckley could not have been prouder of its famous buzzards if every one of them was a peacock.

Meanwhile, the unconcerned vultures go about their age-old business of roosting on the limestone ledges and rearing their unattractive young in the nearby woods. They ordinarily lay their eggs in May or early June, even earlier in southern states, and they lay them on the ground or a rocky ledge and make no effort to construct a nest.

From a vulture's point of view his is not a bad life. He travels effortlessly by air and goes where he wants when he pleases. Like man, he has practically no enemies except man. The vulture is a bird of unfettered independence. He asks no help and seeks no love. Even in Hinckley, where vultures find surprising affection, it's a one-sided affair. Vultures just aren't accustomed to being loved.

# TEN

# Congratulate the Redwing

These are good times for the dashing, carefree red-winged blackbird. In recent years his numbers have built up to phenomenal levels. His famed "oka-lee" song rising from cattail marsh and alfalfa meadow sounds for all the world like, "Happy Days Are Here Again."

Anyone who talks of harming the redwing, even a farmer who has fed them half his corn crop, is often subject to cold looks and sharp words. The redwing has been immortalized in song and nursery rhyme. He's close to the hearts of millions of people. He adds a dash of color to the outdoors and a monotonous but melodious song to field and marshland. Those who hunt and fish or farm the fields have long known him as close companion and have taken special notice of his dashing, band-master's uniform.

In moderate numbers the redwing is warmly welcomed, but the more prevalent he becomes the cooler the greeting he is given. Now there is wide agreement that the redwings have simply gone too far, so leading scientists across the nation have consolidated their attack on what has become known as "the blackbird problem."

Untold millions of blackbirds feast on Arkansas rice, Arizona sorgums, California fruits, Ohio sweet corn, and Texas truck crops. They invade and destroy holly groves in Washington, and all across the country they swarm into cattle feedlots and consume millions of pounds of costly feed meant to go into beefsteak instead.

So serious have blackbirds become to farmers around the southwestern corner of Ohio that corn growers organized a vigilante committee to deal with them. Calling themselves the Whitewater Farmer's Protective Association this group of pioneering farmers held meetings, consulted with state and federal bird specialists, and helped in efforts to trap and poison the offending corn consumers. But like bird-plagued farmers almost everywhere, the Whitewater Farmer's Protective Association has lost every round.

One truck gardener from California's Imperial Valley said that in thirty years of farming, he had coped successfully with all manner of insects and

diseases. "But I have seen my lettuce crop destroyed completely, sometimes overnight," he added sadly, "by swarms of blackbirds. It's one menace we can't cope with. We need help from the federal government."

The federal government was ready to come to grips with the blackbirds. To begin with, officials tried to determine the annual cost to the American farmer of this unwelcome pecking. "When we add it up," said one member of the U. S. House Committee on Agriculture, who was also an Arkansas farmer, "the total is so large we don't want to use it. Nobody would believe it."

In his own state of Arkansas, he added, blackbirds consume 5½ million dollars worth of farm crops, mostly rice, every year. Conservative estimates place the national total at more than 100 million dollars a year lost to the blackbird's appetite.

At the heart of the blackbird problem is the fact that redwings are engaged in a population explosion. It has been going on for several years. One estimate credits them with a twenty percent increase in a recent three-year period. No one knows how many blackbirds there are. "But I can't help thinking," said Dr. M. L. Giltz, the Ohio Agricultural Experiment Station's nationally known authority on redwings, "that their numbers are increasing each year."

As a result of this extensive research, we have learned a few discomforting facts about the red-winged blackbird and his life, loves, and travels.

In one Wisconsin study area the males begin to arrive for the breeding season in March. They stay around until August or September. The male bird stakes out his territory when he first comes into a marsh. Within this territory he has three or four females who have subterritories of their own. In unladylike fashion they fight to keep other females out. Redwings have their best nesting success in wet years because they build a wet nest.

Usually each female brings off a single brood of four or five young. As soon as the family is old enough the blackbirds become wanderers. The males and females split into separate flocks and take separate vacations until the following spring. The drab females look so much different from their males that some farmers consider them a separate species and sometimes call them "rice birds."

As fall approaches the flocks increase in size. Other kinds of blackbirds join redwings. Of an evening you see great wispy flocks of blackbirds shifting like smoke against the distant horizon as the multitudes return to their roosting areas in marshes and woodlands. In time these flocks depart. There is a constant shifting; the redwings spend the winter south of their nesting region.

One reason for the red-winged blackbird's prosperity lies in the bird's ability to adapt his nesting habits to man's farming practices. This historic inhabitant of the cattail marshes has become adapted

to nesting in the fields of alfalfa which cover growing acreages of our farm lands. There may be as
many as six nests in a single acre of alfalfa.

Farmers, besieged by hordes of migrating blackbirds, have tried an amazing list of devices to preserve their crops.

Scarecrows, historic answer to marauding birds,
have taken all manner of forms, from traditional
straw men to strips of feed sacks tied across the
corn rows to wave in the breeze. But the blackbirds
ignore them. When one Ohio corn grower witnessed
the pests descending on his fields, he decided to
dynamite the trees in which they roosted. "Only the
bare branches were left," he said, "after I set off the
dynamite." What about the blackbirds? "The next
day," he added, "those bare branches were covered
with new blackbirds."

Airplanes have been used to buzz flocks of blackbirds feeding on ripening corn. Daring pilots, flying
at tassle-top levels have tried to round up flocks of
corn-eating birds and drive them from the fields.
But the birds simply drop deeper among the corn
stalks.

Other farmers perch on raised platforms and
shoot into the flocks with .22 caliber rifles to keep
the birds moving. Such measures are legal where
blackbirds are causing damage. One farmer riding
along the edge of his corn field spied a flock of
blackbirds settling. He screeched to a halt and got
off a fast rifle shot right through the car window—

before he realized that he hadn't opened it.

Legislators besieged by blackbird-hating voters were delighted a few years ago when the anti-blackbird forces came up with a giant, light trap designed to lure great flocks off their roosts and into captivity. The device did work with some success in various localities. But mile-wide clouds of shifting blackbirds soon replenished any local losses.

When all proper debts are laid at the blackbird's door, there is little room for argument. But most of the year and over most of the land he is harmless and sometimes, where he eats weed seeds and insects, even helpful. It is the redwing's gregariousness that causes us trouble.

While we raise funds and grope for answers, the blackbirds rally their number. Through it all the redwing, fabled in song and rhyme, taunts us cheerfully with his age-old "oka-lee."

What this country needs is a better scarecrow!

# ELEVEN

# Over the Hills with the Foxhounds

Hughes Atkinson was out feeding his ten foxhounds the last time I stopped by his mountaintop home. To reach Atkinson's beef, sheep, and tobacco farm, you wind down the valley out of Owingsville, Kentucky, and double back up the ridge until you can look out over half of Bath County.

This is foxhound country, where fox chasing is an old and honored sport. Participants sit around a glowing fire atop a hill all night listening to the cry of the pack as it trails the red fox through the valleys and over the hills. They talk of the chase that is in progress and the order of the baying hounds on the trail. "Listen," one of them will say as he stares off

FOXHOUND

into the night. "Hear that? Old John's leadin' again. Can't miss that deep choppin' mouth." Usually it's old John's owner who says it.

These men are not out to kill the fox. They would rather he lived to run another night. Some of them even insist that the fox enjoys the chase as much as the hounds. As evidence they point out that he will pass den after den and never hole up unless pushed too hard by the hounds. Every foxhound, whether Walker, Trigg, July, or Goodman, has its fans.

Hughes Atkinson was unofficial historian of a variety of foxhound known as the Goodman. I've never seen owners more sold on their dogs than those who own Goodman hounds.

"Lot of people don't know that Goodman is the best foxhound," Atkinson told me.

I had to admit that I couldn't tell one kind from the other. All of them are big, rangy hounds with a wide variety of coloring and sad but proud faces. "All you gotta do if you can't tell 'em apart," he said, "is run 'em together. The one that comes out ahead is the Goodman. When it comes to runnin', the Goodman has other hounds chained to a post."

This kind of talk gets immediate agreement from other Goodman owners. One of them once told me that with a Goodman hound on the trail, a fox "doesn't stay in one place long enough to shine light on."

There are many classic dog stories told among the men who own hounds and chase foxes. But one of the hardest stories to explain involves a Goodman female called Hightail. I heard the story a few years ago from an Illinois farmer who has raised dozens of Goodman hounds.

Hightail was born in Indiana. In her fourth year she was shipped to Virginia to raise a couple of litters of pups. She was there for several years and while there she was hit by an automobile. The accident left old Hightail deaf, blind in one eye, and with a caved-in place in one side of her head.

Even so, my informant wanted her sent out from Virginia to Illinois to raise another litter of fine foxhounds. This brought Hightail within 120 miles of her birthplace, which she had left many years earlier. She disappeared almost at once. A few nights later Hightail showed up in Indiana. She came up in the night to her original owner, who was out, as one might have guessed, chasing foxes. What guided old Hightail over 120 miles of unknown trails back to her birthplace, which she hadn't seen for years, is something no dog owner can explain. Some can't even believe it!

Another story you can hear from dog owners down in Kentucky's fox-chasing country is about the Kentuckian who moved westward to Missouri. He took with him a pack of Robinson hounds tied to the rear axle of his wagon. A few weeks later a cousin found one of the hounds outside when he went out to do the evening chores. The dog had even crossed the Mississippi River to get back home.

Hughes Atkinson told me of still another fox-hound (Goodman, of course) that arrived at her new destination at four o'clock in the afternoon after a fifty-mile train trip. She escaped and before morning made the return trip on foot. And Goodman owners think she probably took time out to chase a few foxes on the way.

# TWELVE

# Watchbird in the Barnyard

Once when I must have been approaching the ripe age of eight, our family packed up all our belongings and moved to a new farm, thus introducing me to another world that needed exploring. I no longer recall what treasures were left behind by the previous family with the exception of a welcoming committee composed of a flock of eight guinea fowl. As time wore on we decided that the guinea fowl had been left not as a present but as "good riddance."

My brother and I discovered the birds first and raced back to the house to report the windfall to our parents. We had never before owned guineas and only recognized them from having seen them on a

few farms and at the county fair, where they were
displayed in chicken-wire boxes.

We were so breathless when we dashed into the
house that Dad stopped in the middle of the empty
living room and stood there looking at us over the
high back of a rocking chair he had carried in. "Out
behind the barn," my brother gasped, "we found
some guineas. A whole bunch of guineas." I wondered why the revelation did not excite my father
as it had us. Instead of looking happy Dad stood
there holding the rocking chair and slowly shaking
his head the way he did when a hog died.

As I grew older I realized that a good portion of
the farms that had guineas probably got them the
same way. They came with the place. On moving
day you could always catch the hogs, cow, mule,
dog, and as many cats as you wanted. You would
catch up the chickens the night before. But the
guineas were another matter. They were wary, alert,
suspicious, and elusive.

Our flock of eight guineas or their descendants
lived with us as long as we were on that farm. When
we moved we left them for the next family. One
kindness deserves another. And besides that, Dad
never was certain we really owned those birds.

The guinea fowl seems completely unconcerned
by the fact that his success on American farms has
never rivaled that of the turkey or leghorn hen.
Guineas are scattered mostly in small flocks on
farms here and there, with a few larger producers

GUINEA FOWL

raising them commercially for the fancy restaurant trade. As tablefare they rate high. The meat resembles pheasant or quail and is a delicacy in fine restaurants. Chickens multiplied into the millions as the land was settled, and turkeys were domesticated and raised by numbers that still skyrocket. Through the years the guinea has stubbornly refused to let man remodel him, which may help account for the fact that he is still relegated to minority status in the barnyard. We have changed the contours of the turkey, the shape of the market hog, and the conformation of the cow. But the guinea fowl displays genetic stubbornness and an unbending personality. In exchange for the privilege of eating cracked corn with the chickens, he consents to live around the barnyard. You must accept him for what he is, which is what he was a long time ago.

The guinea fowl is a beetle-shaped bird with a little naked head sticking up on one end and not much of a tail sticking out on the other. In the African brush various kinds of guinea fowl still run wild. Those found on farms are of three main colorations, white, pearl, and lavender. Those left behind on our farm were the pearl-colored birds. They wore a plumage of dark, bluish feathers dappled with white polka dots. Most of the larger flocks kept today for the commercial markets are of the white variety. The lavender guinea fowl is light gray with white polka dots. And that's about it! Take it or leave it; it's all the same to the guinea.

But this strange bird has his staunch defenders, and at the drop of a feather they tick off a long list of points in his favor. "You will not," they insist, "find a better watchdog anywhere." Not that the guinea is a fighter; he simply turns in the alarm. Given the slightest excuse, and sometimes none at all, the strident voices of these squat, wary birds pierce the country air with cries that carry to the next farm. The cry of alarm is raised with equal force at the passing of a hawk, visit of a salesman, or a piece of paper blowing across the yard. Many a guinea owner has considered this bird worthwhile because it alerts turkeys and chickens to approaching danger.

The guinea is a rugged, disease-resistant bird. He is welcome in many a garden because he wanders up and down the rows feeding greedily on all the insects he can find and, unlike the chicken, is not given to scratching.

Guineas possess great skill in hiding their nests. The best plan for finding one is to watch for the male bird because he stands guard as his mate incubates the eggs. By removing the eggs as she begins to lay you may increase the number of eggs she will produce. Some guinea hens have been known to lay 125 eggs in a season, no matter for pride among leghorns perhaps, but not bad for a bird as independent as the guinea.

The incubated eggs hatch in twenty-eight days. Within a month or so the young are ready to wander about the farm and gather much of their own food.

And by the time they're two months old, they're big enough to begin roosting in the top of the old Winesap tree or even the great sycamore down by the creek and, like their parents, cry out in alarm at the slightest provocation. At this age too, they are old enough to be eaten, which is a good idea—if you can catch them.

THIRTEEN

# See
# No
# Weevil

In the early part of the Gay Nineties there came across the Rio Grande a little immigrant destined to bring trials and tribulations to the cotton growers in this country. From the human's point of view the eating habits of this creature were unfortunate. All it wanted was cotton. And so rapidly did the cotton boll weevil spread that in some years it damaged the cotton crop to the tune of three million dollars.

This is a lot of eating for insects so small that it takes four of them to equal an inch. But the boll weevil can take pride in the fact that at least one cotton-growing community erected a statue to it.

The statue stands today in Enterprise, Alabama.

It was erected to commemorate what the boll weevils did to the cotton crop of 1910. They ruined it. Desperate farmers turned eventually to planting soybeans where the cotton had grown. The substitute crops prospered and times got better. The longer people thought about it, the more they were convinced they owed gratitude to the boll weevil. "In profound appreciation," says the plaque on the monument, "to the boll weevil and what it has done to herald prosperity."

The boll weevil, however, could not interpret this development as a widespread victory. He has been, after all, the worst insect pest ever to attack the cotton crop, and farmers engage in relentless combat against him.

The invasion of the boll weevil started at Brownsville, Texas. His advances covered about 20,000 square miles a year in the following three decades, and on some of the best of cotton lands production fell from two bales an acre to a bale for every fifteen acres. By 1922 he had spread all the way to Virginia.

The four stages in the life of a boll weevil are egg, larva, pupa and adult. The adult is an unimpressive looking creature with a tiny, dome-shaped, brownish body, moving along on six spindly legs. Out front is a snout like a tiny punch and on its end is the mouth of the insect, a sharp little cutter bar.

In winter the adult boll weevils spend their time dormant, hidden in weeds or trash, usually near a cotton patch. Then in early summer when the cotton

is beginning to prosper, the boll weevils come out of hiding. They feed on the flower buds or "squares" and the young cotton bolls and leave little puncture marks as evidence of their visits. Unlike the gruff papa bear who asked, "Who's been eating from my bowl," the weevil is not particular.

Then the females begin the serious business of laying their eggs. The female does not lay eggs in the cotton boll. Instead she insists on leaving her treasure in the squares. Pioneering scientists working with the insect did not understand this. If they had, the boll weevil might have been named the "square weevil." But by any name it would be equally unwelcome except perhaps in Enterprise, Alabama.

The general rule is one egg to the square. But that's all it takes. The female cruises over the square, and if it is uninfested by any of her kind she corrects the oversight. She peels back the outer layer and eats a deep hole into the square. Then she turns and tenderly places her egg at the bottom of the well and fills the hole with a fluid sealing wax as protection. It's a neat job. But considering the practice boll weevils have had, it should be.

The little white egg, scarcely one twenty-fifth of an inch long, is not pretty like the blue egg of the robin or camouflaged like that of the killdeer, but it holds great potential. Within four days, if conditions are good, the egg opens and the larva emerges.

The tiny grub goes right to work. Now he must

eat fast. Otherwise the rapidly growing cotton plant may crush him. But the square in which the larva lives will not develop into a cotton ball. When a cotton grower finds the deformed squares lying on the ground, he has mute evidence of the boll weevil's presence.

In another seven to fourteen days the grub changes into a pupa. And in three to five more days it has undergone amazing transformations and become a fully equipped adult boll weevil. Quickly cutting itself a tunnel, it comes out into the warm Dixie sunlight. In the brief span of three weeks it has graduated from egg to adult.

The best of leghorn hens cannot approach the egg-laying record of a female boll weevil, which can lay half-a-dozen eggs a day. It was not intelligence that brought success to the boll weevil. Scientists tell us that the male doesn't even recognize the female until they are within an inch of each other.

Skilled scientists have long searched for better ways to kill the cotton pickin' insect and put an end to his foraging in the fibers. The latest control methods for the cotton boll weevil are divided into two plans: one employing cultural practices, the other chemical insecticides. If the cultural practices work well enough, the chemicals may not be needed.

One major way to shortstop the boll weevil is to reduce the number of adults going into the winter. The U. S. Department of Agriculture outlines rules for such a campaign. Choose rapid fruiting, early maturing varieties of cotton adapted to your area, says the Department. Harvest the crop and destroy the plants as early as possible. Practice clean cultivation. Mow the ditch banks and clean out the thickets, especially those near the cotton fields. This way you help deprive the adult weevils of wintering quarters. Then the following season, if boll weevils show up, start early with a program of chemical control. Either that or give up and build a statue.

# FOURTEEN

# *Honking Watchdog*

Barnyard geese for all their virtues lead an uncertain life. They can't tell from one unmusical honk to the next what fate may befall them. Through the ages their owners have periodically attacked them in strange fashion.

They have pulled feathers to make writing pens, harvested the soft down to keep themselves warm, and shamelessly robbed geese's nests of their most valued treasures. It's little wonder that geese so treated resent the repeated assaults on their dignity. Some say that geese, notoriously mean, aren't mean until they get the idea from man.

Consider, for example, goose-plucking day on my grandfather's farm. Before the age of synthetic fibers and electric blankets, farm people needed those goose feathers to make pillows and soft, warm quilts. Once a year Grandma had to pick from each bird that pound of feathers which a prime goose will produce in a year.

Grandpa, with yellow corn and loud yelling, would herd the complaining geese into an enclosure. One at a time we'd catch them and stretch them out for Grandma. She would slip a stocking over their heads as a blinder and my brother and I would hold down the wings, legs, and neck as though we had a tiger by the tail. It was never an easy day for geese or people.

The goose that gets picked has it easy compared to the goose that gets "noodled." "Noodling" is limited largely to southern Europe. The birds are kept in small, dark pens and force fed by hand on cooked dough noodles several times a day. They make magnificent gains in body weight. Their livers grow especially big and are prized for *paté de foie gras*. No wonder geese are mean.

In spite of the fact that geese account for only two-tenths of one percent of American poultry, there's hardly anyone with a farm background who doesn't have at least one story to tell about a mean gander. Our neighbors back home had an old white Embden gander so mean we called him "Billy the Kid."

When I went to school I had to pass Billy the Kid. This was never easy. True to his namesake, this big

gander had fast reactions, a sharp eye, and a deadly
aim. He also had the neck of a snake, the temper
of a mule, the jaws of a 'gator and the fearlessness
of a nursing sow. He thought I was afraid of him—
and I was!

The showdown between us came one day when
we were both seven years old. Billy the Kid outran
me and attacked from the rear. He attached his beak
firmly to the back of my trousers. With his viselike
grip he clamped down and tore the whole seat out
of my blue jeans.

But life for a gander is more than a running battle
with those who have domesticated him. He deports
himself with dignity and looks the whole world
squarely in the eye. And well he might, because he
does possess some talents.

He needs only grass and water to eat, gets along
without shelter and largely takes care of himself.
He's even a better watchdog than most dogs are.
The Romans knew this a couple of thousand years
ago. Inside the city walls they kept a flock of sacred
geese which sounded the alarm that aroused the
guards who beat back the invading Gauls. The geese
were credited with saving Rome. It was a day of
glory for geese!

Once mated geese stay mated, something of a
model for the animal world. There are several
breeds of them—Embden, African, Toulouse, Chinese, Egyptian, White Roman, and a few others. In
all but the Pilgrim goose the sexes look alike, so

much so it almost takes a member of the flock to tell who's who. Geese have changed little through the ages. And we assume that meets with the approval of geese.

Geese won a new degree of respect some years ago when farmers in Tennessee and West Virginia discovered that they would weed strawberry patches without damaging the money crop. Geese are the closest grazing of all domesticated animals. Experiment stations conducted economic studies about the goose in the strawberry patch. After some months of counting, measuring, weighing, and adding things up they figured that a goose flock is worth an extra fifty dollars an acre to the strawberry grower.

The goose, known now as the "berry farmer's hired hand," suddenly found new popularity. The call went out. There weren't enough geese to pull all the waiting weeds. Now one goose producer in the Southwest grows a quarter million geese a year. And while many of them go to cities for employment in meat markets, from 50,000 to 100,000 are shipped off to Arkansas and Louisiana for more pleasant and permanent work in the berry patches. It's good to see men and geese cooperating.

# FIFTEEN

# Owl, They Say, That Screeches

Screech owls, *Otus asio,*
are probably the best known of all American owls
in spite of the fact that they are seldom seen. They
are close neighbors of most of us and their doleful,
quavering calls fill the night. Various subspecies are
found in almost all of the United States as far north
as southern Alaska.

Screech owls may stand ten inches high and are
the only small owls with ear tufts. They come in two
colors. There are the gray ones and the reddish
brown. This color difference apparently has nothing to do with sex, age, food habits or style-
consciousness. In fact, no one is sure what it does
have to do with. The color difference, however, does

SCREECH OWL

not worry the screech owls. They mix freely. One parent may be red, the other gray, and the young either color.

A screech owl that I once kept in captivity, by special permit, for photographic purposes, revealed the color of his plumage from the time his wing feathers started to show. From the time he was quite young, he could make sharp, clicking noises if disturbed. He did this by snapping his lower mandible against the rigid upper mandible. If you approached his cage and disturbed him, he would click several times in solemn warning. If he tried to fly from one perch to another and missed, he would sit on the cage floor, a bit ruffled, and click at himself. Naturally enough, his name was "Clicker."

Before Clicker had been in captivity long he developed another sound. This was a low volume, contented twittering that he sometimes kept up for hours.

Obtaining food for the growing young screech owl presented problems. He ate amazing quantities each night. When half-grown he could easily consume a sparrow or large mouse, then take an offering of insects to top it off. Hamburger from the butcher shop would not suffice. The feathers, bone, and hair that owls normally get with their food seem to be essential to them. So like the parent owls, I scoured the countryside. I became adept at watching the roadsides for freshly killed birds or mammals. I paid neighborhood boys a nickel for each mouse they delivered to the door.

By leaving the outside lights on, I could attract enough beetles and moths to satisfy Clicker's hunger momentarily. His first living prey was a medium-sized moth I put into his cage. He opened his gaping mouth and snapped his head forward so fast the moth had no chance to escape.

He had trouble at first with the hard-shelled June bugs. I offered him one of the big brown beetles by simply dropping it into his cage. The insect fell on its back and lay there buzzing loudly in futile efforts to right itself. The little owlet cocked his head to one side, looked at the beetle and, at last, lunged and grabbed it as a self-respecting screech owl should. This was perhaps the first time he held live prey in his talons. In due time Clicker was released and permitted to return to the wild.

The list of foods known to appeal to screech owls is long and sometimes amazing. They consume all manner of small birds, sometimes catching them in the air or on the perch and sometimes taking them from the nest. They are death on mice. They most often eat whatever prey is readily available at the moment. If it is little enough to catch and alive enough to move, Heaven help it, because the screech owl knows his work well. He is a predator in spirit and in fact, and performs his assigned role in nature's pyramid with no more feeling over the fate of his prey than the mouse the owl eats has for the beetles it consumes.

Screech owls have been known to take birds as big as grouse and they have frequently caught pigeons. Of 225 stomachs examined in one screech-owl food study several years ago, one owl had eaten a pigeon, 38 had consumed small birds, 91 had dined on mice, 2 had taken lizards, while others had settled for insects, spiders and crawfish; and one had even caught a fish. Yet 43 of the owls, alas, had empty stomachs.

One student of bird life many years ago found a screech owl nest to which the owl had carried 16 catfish. And 4 of the catfish were still alive! Another screech owl entered a home by coming down the chimney. The owl took the pet canary from its cage and consumed it which, for the owl, was the natural thing to do.

If ever a bird was equipped well for his way of life, this is the one. The screech owl moves on silent wings. His big flight feathers are lacy and soft and they make no audible sound as he goes. He can fly on easy wing beats, make abrupt turns in midair or even hover over the spot in the meadow or woodland where he detects movement or sound.

His biggest aids other than his silent flight, say the scientists who have studied the owl's equipment, are his eyes and ears. Both are outstanding mechanisms. Some people estimate that the night-sight of screech owls is a hundred times better than that of man.

The owl's eyes are made to stare straight ahead. This is at least one reason why he turns his head deliberately to follow the movements of anyone walking past him. Old Ben Wright, who lived near us when I was a child, often told me that if I kept walking around an owl, he would turn his head around and around to watch me until he twisted his head off. I believe now that Ben knew better. But an owl can turn his head halfway around. And after a full 180 degrees, he snaps it back an equal distance in the other direction so fast that it seems his head has not changed directions at all.

The ears of the owl are almost as efficient as his eyes. The owl can hear the slight rustle of the grass in the meadow below. It can detect the footsteps of a field mouse.

Clicker taught me that a smaller creature has scant chance of escape once an owl has it in his talons. On each foot the owl is equipped with two pairs of opposing talons. His talons are curving grippers with needle-sharp points. By standing on his prey and holding it firmly in his talons, the screech owl tears his dinner into bite size at his leisure. Table manners mean little. It is common and acceptable practice for him to bolt his food, bones, feathers, hair and all. Later the indigestible portions are regurgitated in pellets. Research people collect owl pellets for clues to the owl's eating habits.

Late in winter, sometimes in February, the screech owls may be heard singing their famous mournful love songs. When I heard my first screech owl ballad I was still quite young. Outside my room in the old farmhouse was a tall rose arbor where every year a screech owl seemed inspired to sing to his love. At the sound of his ghostly call in the darkness, I would slide farther down beneath the covers. In later years I changed my opinion of the screech owl's music. Someone misnamed this owl. He does not screech. His voice has a deep, mellow, and pleasing sound that seems to be a part of the woodlands.

It may well have been hill-country superstition that accounted for the fact that the screech owls frightened me in the first place. These small owls loom large in folklore. There are still those who insist that their call is a sure sign of approaching death. But take heart. There is a way to prevent this disaster, assuming, that is, you awaken and hear the owl. You must arise immediately from your bed, says the old story, and turn the pockets of your pants wrong side out.

In March or April screech owls search out hollow limbs, often in old apple orchards, and there the female lays five or six eggs. She alone incubates the eggs. The chore takes her twenty-six days. But when the young are hatched both parents work to feed them.

Screech owls will savagely defend their families.

It is not at all rare for them to attack humans during this season. Game protectors often get complaints about owls in this period. Let a screech owl knock off the hat of a pedestrian six feet tall, and the irate citizen rushes to his telephone and demands protection. The screech owl means business, all right, but his size is against him. He accomplishes little more than to harass his victims. It seems admirable that a bird so small will challenge a full grown human—unless you happen to be the human under attack.

Just as the screech owl lives by violence, he has many a woodland neighbor that will gladly end his bloody little career. One of these is the great horned owl—king of the night. During the daylight hours crows and jays harass the screech owl if he should come out in the open, and they are likely to be joined by a flock of smaller birds that chase the little owl into hiding.

Small wonder that screech owls spend their days in the nest cavity sometimes with their heads sticking warily from the doorway. They may not be looking for trouble, but it won't take them by surprise.

SIXTEEN

# *The Determined Ant*

Men and ants have much in common. It is possible that we may even have learned a thing or two from ants whether we will admit it or not. And well we might, because ants are gifted with talent, blessed with determination, and skilled at organizing their work. Among them are professional baby sitters, soldiers, nurses, butchers, hunters, and scouts. Others, sadly enough, are slaves.

Tastes vary among the ants. Some eat meat, some are strict vegetarians, while some live on milk and honey.

Scientists have devoted lifetimes of study unraveling the innermost secrets of the ants. They estimate that 15,000 species of ants are scurrying over every part of the earth except near the North and South Poles. Ants are the earth's most abundant insects.

Ants, like people, seek out company. They are highly regimented social creatures, and hundreds of thousands of them sometimes live in the same apartment house.

But some ants, such as the army ants of Central America and Africa, are nomads, gypsies that have no permanent home. They wander across the tropical jungle wherever instinct and the search for food leads them. And close behind them may come an entomologist intent on learning how they live. One scientist who has studied them is Dr. T. C. Schnierla. At frequent intervals in a period of thirty years he escaped his laboratory on the fifth floor of New York's big stone American Museum of Natural History to go live with the fierce Eciton ants of Central America. In 1932 on the first of these safaris he slept in a jungle hammock and followed colonies of ants for as long as four months at a time.

"I have seen them kill snakes, lizards and fledgling birds," Dr. Schnierla told me. He has no doubt that they could either sting or smother to death larger animals which are too crippled to flee from their path. "They move as much as 300 feet a day," he said, "sending columns out like the branches of a tree from their main columns."

These are the meat eaters, tracking down, killing,

butchering and carrying home every insect that fails
to escape.

As they move, they flush out hordes of flying insects. These attract the ant birds that live by staying
just ahead of the foraging army ants.

Unless the queen ant is producing a new crop of
eggs, the army ants change their bivouac location
every day. One colony Dr. Schnierla studied traveled seventy miles in four-and-a-half years. Toward
evening each day they begin to build a suspended
living mass of ants. "And this," says Dr. Schnierla,
"is a most interesting thing to watch."

A lead ant comes upon some overhanging ledge
or the limb of a tree. On the end of her legs are
opposing, recurved hooks. She gets a grip and hangs
downward. Other ants nearby do the same thing;
then still more workers begin to crawl over them
and hang below the first ants with their hooks.
Gradually they form a chain of ants that widens into
a column reaching to the ground. The ants support-
ing each other could not let go if they wanted to.
The weight of other ants has them locked in position. Somewhere inside this mass of ants, the queen
is snug and protected from the night air. Workers
have carried along the eggs and nymphs and have
seen that these too are secure for the night. To us
this may seem like a poor way to make camp, but it
has worked for the army ants for 65 million years.
Dr. Schnierla has seen such bivouac columns as tall
as sixty feet.

He found that the female workers in an ant colony divide into different groups by size. Some were little and dainty and charged with light work in the community. The biggest of all had magnificent trophy heads equipped with sickle-shaped mandibles, needle-sharp jaws and poison glands for good measure. These husky females are the warriors that defend the bivouac!

Less bloodthirsty are the harvester ants of our own southwestern states. They send out gleaning parties to bring back grass seeds. The ants eat the seed, then toss out the chaff. They also toss away an occasional good seed, and around the ant nest there may spring up a circular row of their favorite food plants. No wonder men have believed that ants know how to farm.

Some ants keep aphids for "milk" animals. The aphids give off a body fluid which ants drink. The ants protect their aphids from every hazard short of DDT and milk them by stroking their bodies.

Some ants have even become slave masters. The Amazon ant has kept slaves for so long that she is no longer capable of doing her own work. She would perish if she did not capture slaves to help her. This should be a lesson for anyone considering keeping slaves.

Some ants go out to harvest pieces of leaves, then march back home carrying them above their heads like tiny parasols. They store the leaves in the nest and fungus grows on them. And what could be better than mushrooms fresh picked from the home garden?

Ants living in some tropical jungles weave and sew leaves together to build nests. Their nests hang from the limbs of trees. Where do weaver ants get their thread? First they use jaws and legs to pull the edges of leaves close together. Meanwhile a row of workers marches from the nest and every one of them tenderly carries an ant larva between her jaws. An adult ant holds one of the larva up to the matching edges of the leaves. When she gently squeezes it the larva becomes a little sewing machine. It neatly binds leaves together with its special thread.

The Chinese know that these ants are highly warlike. In trees where they live no other insects can survive. So the Chinese cut down the weaver ant nests and carefully hang them in their citrus trees when aphids and other pests threaten the crop. There are even places where ant nests are sold, thereby indicating that man is still one jump ahead of the bugs.

There are three kinds of individuals in an ant colony, the queen, the workers and the males. The queen is the mother of the colony but not the ruler. The worker ants take good care of her and do all the other work besides. Some scientists say the workers like the queen's perfume. She may live fifteen years and during that time lay hundreds of thousands of eggs that keep the colony vigorous.

What are the chances that an ant will become

queen? Infinitesimal! Most ants in any colony are workers, female domestics that neither mate nor lay eggs.

The male ant is shiftless by nature. He has a single purpose in life, to mate with the queen. Once that is accomplished he dies. The queen mates only once in her lifetime.

Life within an ant colony is less peaceful than it looks. Individuals fight constantly. Ants are well built for battle and exceedingly strong for their size. When ants from neighboring bands cross paths they often fight with complete disregard for themselves, killing where they can and dying if they must. The only slackers in the battle of the ants are the males. They are not equipped for such rough play.

Among the female ant's useful equipment are her jaws, which are hinged to work sideways. She may use them to crush a seed or nip at the head of an adversary. It's all in a day's work.

Many kinds of ants can leave trails for others from their colony to follow. Their abdomens touching the ground lay scent tracks. The next time you find a trail of ants crossing a leaf, move the leaf and see what happens. The ants will probably stop where the edge of the leaf was. Scouts will make short exploratory runs in many directions. They move farther and farther until they find the other end of the broken trail and mend it.

Some years ago Dr. Schnierla built a maze in which he put ants to see what they could learn. The insects had to travel the maze to go from food to nest. Some of the alleys in the maze were dead-end streets and some were not. After several tries the ants began going shorter and shorter distances into the dead-end streets. Eventually they ignored them and followed only the true passages. They had memorized landmarks just as any of us might to find our way out of the woods.

This is admirable for an animal so small. In fact, who could blame an ant if it bragged a little?

# SEVENTEEN

# Powerful Woodpecker

The pileated woodpecker was conditioned by nature to be secretive and shy and to avoid the haunts of man. As civilization advanced and the forests disappeared, the pileated woodpeckers went with them. Eventually it began to look as though this magnificent woodpecker, big as a crow and sometimes known among mountain people as the "wood-cock," was doomed. Said naturalist T. Gilbert Pearson, "It is quite possible that he will not long survive the passing of our primeval forests."

But by the time I was tramping the wooded hill country as a boy in southeastern Ohio, I would see an occasional pileated woodpecker dipping and

PILEATED WOODPECKER

gliding from wooded ridge to wooded ridge and calling in loud unmusical tones as he went. Always I stopped to admire his size, his bright red crown, and jet black body with big black wings on which I could see white feathers flashing as he flew. A glimpse of him was a treat anytime.

The pileated woodpecker fooled everyone who said he couldn't adapt to the changes man was making in the landscape. In recent years his numbers have begun to climb again. Outdoorsmen are rejoicing at the big woodpecker's fine comeback. People who never saw one before, now frequently encounter this dashing woodchopper. Sometimes the pileated woodpecker leaves a bad impression on human neighbors.

For example there was the Columbus, Ohio, family awakened at sunrise on a recent spring morning by pounding and ripping sounds that made them believe their house was being torn apart. There on the window sill was a woodpecker and he was throwing chips all around him.

No matter how many times the woodpecker was chased away, he returned to tear off more window sill. With sledgehammer blows he pounded the hard wood. Soon the homeowner called the Columbus Zoo and talked to the curator of birds, who quickly loaded a few mist nets into his car and rushed across town for a closer look at the bird on the window sill. Just as he had hoped, the curator soon determined that it was indeed a pileated woodpecker and, as good fortune would have it, the bird was a male. The woodpecker, enroute to his window sill encountered an almost invisible net and was securely ensnared. An hour later the big bird was slipped into a large cage in the Columbus Zoo where he was greeted nonchalantly by the female already in residence.

Visitors could see them there, providing they could coax them out of the hollow stump in which they spent much of their time. This was one of the few pairs of pileated woodpeckers in captivity anywhere. They ate a mushy offering of ground meat, carrots, dried poultry feed, wheat germ oil, cod liver oil, hard-boiled eggs (complete with shell), and banana. And they seemed perfectly happy in spite of the fact that they were born to live deep in the forest, free of wing and wild of spirit.

As any wild creature might, the pileated woodpecker ran afoul of the plans of man. The demolished window sill is but a minor episode. Think how the rows of utility poles must have looked to the first of these giant woodpeckers to see them.

No one knows quite when the pileated woodpeckers first discovered utility poles, but to the bird, here were rows of dead trees that deserved his attention. He chose one, slapped himself to a stop near its top and braced himself securely with tail and claws. Typical of his clan, he gave a couple of light taps against the pole and turned an ear to listen for wood boring insects therein. Then, the woodpecker set-to with a vigor that would have given one a headache to watch.

As a result something had to be done. Utility company officials set aside a sum of money for researchers at Pennsylvania State College, located in the heart of the pileated woodpecker's stronghold. The scientists were asked to find a way to discourage woodpeckers from feeding on utility poles.

Perhaps they could scare them away. Experimental snakes, fashioned from sections of green garden hose were festooned from the poles. The woodpeckers ignored them. Strips of waving cloth were hung from the wires and the poles. The woodpeckers ignored these too. Eventually test poles were wrapped in chicken wire and company officials took new hope. But the woodpeckers braced themselves, tore away the wire and dropped it to the ground. Then they went right on with their rat-a-tat-tat.

Various chemicals were painted on the poles. "But," as one college official concluded, "anything that would keep woodpeckers off the poles would also keep workmen off."

Perhaps utility company officials would profit by looking into the teachings of those few ornithologists who have studied the life and times of the pileated woodpecker. One of the most thorough studies ever made of this bird was by the late Dr. Southgate Y. Hoyt, a Cornell University ornithologist at Ithaca, New York. Dr. Hoyt had a lasting interest in the big woodpeckers. Says his widow, Dr. Sally F. Hoyt, also an ornithologist, "We were the first to be able to keep one in captivity for more than a month. We had ours for nine and a half years. I want to make a plea to you," said Mrs. Hoyt recently, "please give the birds a break. They are not villains. Every bit of our research proved that they never destroy timber or poles."

What then are they doing up there tearing the trees and poles apart? "They remove carpenter ants," says Mrs. Hoyt, "from wood already infected with these insects, thus preventing their spread to neighboring trees or poles. They are the power company's allies, not their enemies. What is needed," she adds convincingly, "is an insect repellent, not a woodpecker repellent."

The birds' defenders make a good point. Finding enough insects to supply their needs is too difficult a task for them to take time out to pound holes for the fun or devilment of it.

The Hoyts' captive pileated woodpecker became a member of the family during the years they kept her. The big bird would land on Dr. Hoyt's shoulder and eat from his hand. On one of these occasions Dr. Hoyt became, perhaps, the only human ever knocked cold by a pileated woodpecker. The bird playfully pecked him once on the side of the head and Dr. Hoyt lost consciousness; this is some indication of the power behind a pileated woodpecker's beak.

When he first constructed a cage for his captive female pileated, the bird was twenty-eight days old and about ready to fly. He constructed a cage large enough for comfort but small enough to prevent the woodpecker from spreading and possibly breaking her wings. It measured eighteen by eighteen by thirty inches high, and the occupant rapidly adopted it as her home. But from a tender age, she was a home-wrecker in the literal sense. Dr. Hoyt made the cage of angle-iron framework, covered with quarter-inch hardware cloth. The cage was equipped with a hinged door in front and a sliding floor for easy cleaning. In one corner was a partly rotted log for the woodpecker's amusement.

But the bird not contented with pecking wood soon took to wire cutting. "It is amazing," reported Dr. Hoyt in one of his numerous scientific papers on pileated woodpeckers, "how this bird can demolish the wire in short order if she wishes to, not by working on a small hole and gradually enlarging it, but by digging out a circle so that a large piece of the wire would drop out at a time, leaving a large hole."

It wasn't that the big woodpecker wanted out of her cage, the only home she knew. In fact, she was often nervous outside. Once she had cut a hole in the wall big enough for an exit, thus proving she could do it, she sometimes moved to the other side of the cage and made a similar hole there.

The cage lasted for three years with frequent

patching. The bird could and did demolish the metal lathing and old license plates with which Dr. Hoyt patched the box.

"I certainly learned," said Dr. Hoyt, "to respect both the power and the accuracy of the blows of the pileated woodpecker." She would break the wire one strand at a time then move on to the next. Often she would strike the wire one blow on one side then a blow on the other until it snapped, as she apparently knew it would.

During World War II, when traveling about the country from assignment to assignment, Dr. Hoyt carried his pet woodpecker in a wicker basket lined with wire. She became the best traveled pileated woodpecker in recent times.

These woodpeckers have two reasons for drilling holes in trees. One is to gather the boring insects on which they live. The other is to build a nesting cavity. You can easily tell their "diggins" should you come across them in the woods. For getting at wood-boring insects, they dig oblong holes often a foot high, four inches across and sometimes six inches deep. They cut them with a vengeance. After a couple of initial tuning up raps, their pounding mounts in volume and force until they're throwing three- or four-inch chips with every two or three blows. You can sometimes hear the pounding across a mile of woodlands.

They light on a tree that appears sound and with uncanny accuracy go right to the heart of the colony of ants. Once they've opened up the cavity the woodpeckers can pull the ants back to their mouths one after the other with their long probing tongues.

Perhaps this tongue is the most amazing of all the pileated woodpecker's equipment. He can extend it as far as three-and-a-half inches past the tip of his beak and bend it in any direction from any point and reach insects around a corner. The tongue is covered with a thick saliva which ensnares insects and holds them until they can be brought back to the bird's mouth.

Excavating for a nesting site may require a month of digging, with the male bird doing most of the work. The nest site is often on a high dead tree. Once completed, the nest cavity may be six to twenty-six inches deep. The birds customarily dig a new cavity each time they make a nest.

Here four or five glossy white eggs are deposited. The male bird is not yet finished with his share of the family duties. He takes over for much of the brooding and incubates the eggs at night. Meanwhile his mate rests snug and untroubled in some other tree cavity in the woods nearby.

A young pileated woodpecker is, by human standards, an ugly creation. But by the time it is twenty-six days old it resembles the parents. The family stays together while the young birds learn how to chop wood for their dinner. Parents and young may stay together into early winter. Then the young birds spread out to find new territories that are short on pileated woodpeckers.

These woodpeckers seldom bother to migrate with the coming of winter. One kept in captivity withstood temperatures ranging from 15 degrees below zero to 117 above without noticeable harm.

There was a time when the pileated woodpecker was considered a game bird and could be purchased at the market. They are said to have a strong flavor and their ant diet must be largely responsible. But even if the pileated woodpecker understood this, it is doubtful that he would alter his eating habits.

# EIGHTEEN

# The
# Unlovely
# Bat

Bats are everywhere, or nearly so. Some two thousand species of them inhabit much of the world. Caves, cliffs, trees and the works of man house them. Because of the homes men have built all over the globe, bats enjoy better accommodations today than ever before. They may live closer to you than you realize. They join you for an evening cookout and dart around you in the failing light, or they fly the insect patrol above you as you fish the edge of a lake or stream.

One of the most unusual experiences I ever had with bats came one dark evening as I cast a fly over a favorite hole in a southern Ohio stream noted for its smallmouthed bass. On one backcast the line grew suddenly heavy. I fought the weight on the line to make a couple of faltering casts to see what was dragging on the hook. As the bait came past my head, I saw a bat struggling against it. Hopefully, I dropped him into the water on the chance a big bass might rise to take him. But brown bat or dry fly the fish were having none of my offerings that night. I released the unhappy bat which was, I assume, considerably shaken to find an insect capable of such a fight.

In all the world of nature there are few creatures that can approach the bat in flying skill. He's so skilled that he can turn, twist, hover, dart, and dive with a mobility that is wonderful and amazing. Bats were first rate aerialists 60 million years before man got off the ground in anything higher than a coconut tree. Wilbur and Orville Wright's efforts on that sandy strip in North Carolina must have looked feeble indeed to the bats maneuvering above them.

Few if any birds can match the flying skill of the bat. And among their fellow mammals, the bat's sole contender for honors in the world of flight is the flying squirrel, who doesn't fly at all but, try as he will, can only glide.

If you ever tried to knock down a flying bat with a broom, you can understand why biologists studying bats prefer to capture them while they sleep. Recently I accompanied Woodrow Goodpaster, who is an authority on bats, on one of his bat-banding expeditions. On a sweltering July day we crawled up beneath the roof of an old barn in southern Ohio. The bats, able to crawl through a half-inch crack, had worked their way up under the boards against the metal roof.

On the flat bed of a hay wagon Woody set up his laboratory scales. He spread out some note sheets, a ruler and equipment for banding bats should he come across any that weren't already wearing bands on their forearms. He had been studying this bat colony for five years.

Now he took those he caught one at a time and checked them carefully to see whether they had gained in weight or length since he inspected them a week ago. During the summer, when the young bats are growing, he checks their rate of growth once a week.

Here at close range I could see the apparatus which gives the bats their amazing powers of flight. The fleshy membrane which keeps them airborne so effortlessly reaches from wrist to ankle, directly across to the tail, then, the other ankle and back to the opposite wrist. The bat's body is almost surrounded by wings.

He is covered with short, mouselike fur and his stub-nosed face has tiny, beady eyes and a mouth that seems too large for him. His eyes are of little value; his sight is limited. More important is his amazing power of hearing. Laboratory tests have shown time and again that you can blindfold bats, release them in a room filled with suspended wires and see them dart through and around the wires almost as easily as when their eyes are not covered.

You can plug their ears, and they begin to bump into obstacles in a helpless fashion. And this takes the discussion quite normally into one of the most amazing bits of animal lore anywhere.

Bats find their way through the dark in and around branches of trees and other obstacles by a highly developed system of sonar. They send out high pitched sounds in voices well beyond the range of the human ear. With their sharply attuned ears they pick up the echoes of the sounds they send, and the echoes tell them when they're approaching an obstacle. By the same system, they also locate much of their flying food. They can track down a hapless moth or beetle on the wing by listening to the echoes that bounce off him. Even in the total darkness of caves where they roost, bats get around with amazing agility and freedom from collision.

But bats, like the rest of us, have their off days when they find it difficult to miss the laboratory wires. Commercial pest-control workers know this well. One of their methods of reducing the bat population when called to the attic of a frantic housewife is to take along a small tree limb from which they have stripped the leaves. They get the bats confused and whizzing around through the attic. Then they begin batting practice. At close range they can knock many of them down.

Easier than batting them down is to watch the building for several evenings and determine what time they go out to dinner. Then locate their entrances and seal them. In northern parts of the country, the best season to seal a building against bats is during the cold months while the migrating bats are down south for the winter.

Wherever they go most bats depend on a diet of insects, which they consume in great numbers. A bat that lives to fifteen years, and they have been known to reach such an age, may eat 100 pounds of insects. He can easily eat in a half-hour's airborne feeding enough insects to equal a third to a half of his body weight.

His usual procedure is to catch insects in his mouth, but sometimes he will drop the membrane between his ankles and scoop up the insects as he swoops over them. Thus caught in the bat's little butterfly net, the hapless insect is bitten in the head and dispatched. Meanwhile the bat's big ears are already attuned to the next course.

Naturalists have discovered at least two species of bats that fish for a living. For a bat to take a fish from the water is no slight accomplishment. These fishing bats are found in Central and South America. One of them does his fishing along the shores of the Gulf of California, and sometimes he will rest during the day beneath loose stones along the saltwater beaches there.

A still better known fishing bat is one called

*Noctilio*, which is found all the way from Mexico to the southern part of the South American continent. Naturalists for the past hundred years have known that *Noctilio* could catch fish up to three or four inches long; they saw him in the act. Later they examined his stomach contents to be certain they were seeing right. But until recently they were never quite sure just how *Noctilio* went about taking fish from the waters.

Then a researcher answered the puzzling question by getting the fishing bats to take fish from a shallow pan in his laboratory. As they swooped down over the water, cameras photographed their methods. The movies solved the mystery. Instead of netting the fish, the bat, at the final approach, folded his net and used his sharp claws as gaff hooks to help him grab a fish and lift it quickly to his mouth.

Of all the bats, the blood sucking vampires, none of which live in the United States, are the most feared. These bats with razor sharp teeth light on sleeping animals, sometimes including man, and so gently do they make their approach and their incision, that the victim seldom awakens while the bat feeds. They spread diseases, especially rabies, through herds of livestock. Reports out of South America say that more than a million head of livestock were lost to rabies in 1956 because of vampire bats.

There are in India, Australia, and some other

countries species of bats called "flying foxes" which live on a diet of fruit. Their taste for peaches, plums, bananas, and apples seems more acceptable to the human being than does the diet of the vampire bats —unless you happen to be an orchardist.

The habits of bats seem strange indeed. Here is a mammal that hangs upside down to sleep or bear its young. Its body temperature goes down with the falling thermometer almost to the freezing point. And when the female bat flies she may carry her young along. Meanwhile, other female bats simply hang their young ones up in the rafters by the hooked toes of their hind feet.

The bat is not so dirty and louse ridden as some would lead us to think. Actually, he is a clean creature who bathes himself at frequent intervals. Human beings have spread other unfair rumors about bats, although it is apparently true that they can carry rabies. It's not true, however, that bats come from little brown eggs. They come, understandably enough, from little brown bats.

And, in spite of what your long-haired aunt may tell you, bats do not make conscious efforts to entangle themselves in a woman's hair. No bat wants to strangle himself to death. If this should happen it is an accident—pure and calamitous and probably as frightening to the bat as to the woman.

As the weather grows colder and the days shorter, some species of bats living in cold climates begin to move southward. The following spring they retrace their paths to the old haunts. Meanwhile, other species spend their winters hibernating.

People engaged in bat research have banded them and moved them about the country to see if they return to home caves and buildings. This has demonstrated that bats possess amazing homing instincts. One shipment of bats caught in Cincinnati, Ohio, was taken to Atlanta, Georgia, and released. Soon they were finding their way back to Cincinnati and to the same building from which they were taken. The numbered aluminum bands on their forearms were positive identification.

Another shipment of bats was sent to Dallas, Texas, with an airline worker who released the bats when his plane landed. They found their way home to the attic of the old Public Library building in the village of Milford, Ohio.

Take another look at the bats flying over your yard. These are mammals of mystery. While recent research has revealed some facts concerning the life of the bat, there is still much about them that we do not understand.

And so it is with all the animals that live in and beyond the barnyard.

# INDEX

Africa, ants of, 112
Agriculture, United States Department of, 95-96
Aldrin, 36
American Milk Goat Registry Association, 30
American Museum of Natural History, 112
Ants, 111-17: Amazon, 114; army, 112-14; carpenter, 123; diet of, 111, 112-13; Eciton, 112-14; egg-laying of, 113; farming, 114; harvester, 114; learning ability of, 116-17; male, 115-16; milking, 114; nests of, 115; olfactory sense of, 116-17; parasol, 114; queen, 113, 115; slave-keeping, 114; society of, 111-12; species of, 112; warrior, 114; weaver, 115; worker, 113-14, 115-16
Aphids, 114
Arsenic, 36
Atkinson, Hughes, 81-84
Audubon, John James, 67-68
Australia, bats of, 134-35

Baltimore orioles, 53
Barro Colorado Islands, Panama, 68
Bass, 56
Bats, 129-36: blood-sucking vampire, 134; capture of, 130; control of, 132-33; description of, 131-32; diet of, 133-34, 135; as disease spreaders, 134-35; fishing, 133-34; habits of, 135; hearing of, 131-32; hibernation of, 136; homing instincts of, 136; metabolism of, 135-36; migration of, 133, 135-36; sight of, 131; species of, 129; superstitions about, 135
Birds, see Cowbirds; Geese; Great

horned owls; Guinea Fowl; Pigeons; Red-winged blackbirds; Screech Owls; Vultures; Woodpeckers, pileated
Blackbirds, see Cowbirds; Redwinged blackbirds
Black vultures: description of, 64, 66; as predators, 67
Bluegills, 56
Border collies, 39-42: intelligence of, 40-42; as pets, 40
Bordner, Robert, 70-71
Bradford, Carl, 40-42
Brownsville, Texas, 92
Buffalo birds, see Cowbirds
Bullfrogs, 56
Bullheads, 56
"Buzzard Sunday," 69-72
Buzzards, see Vultures
Byers, George W., 15-16

Caesar, 51
California, Gulf of, 133
California condors, 66
Capistrano, swallows of, 70
Carver, George Washington, quoted on mules, 24
Cattle: English, 46; industry, 46, 48 (see also Texas longhorns)
Central America: ants of, 112-14; bats of, 133
Chapman, Dr. Frank M., 68
Chaucer, Geoffrey, quoted on goats, 29
Chickens, 49, 88
Chisholm Trail, 46
Cleveland Press, 70-71
Collies, see Border collies
Columbus Zoo, 120-21
Condor, see California condor
Congress, United States, 35-36, 46
Cornell University, 122
Coronado, 46

Cotton boll weevil, *see* Weevils
Cotton crop damage, 91-92
Cowbirds, 13-19: description of,
13-14; diet of, 14; egg-laying
of, 13, 14-16; habits of, 13,
14-16, 18-19; incubation of,
16-18
Crawfish, 55-62: age of, 60; characteristics of, 55-56; description of, 56-57; diet of, 59; egg-
laying of, 59-60; farming of,
58-59; as food, 56-58; molting
of, 60-62; population of, 58;
young of, 60-62

DDT, 114
Dogs, *see* Border collies; Fox-
hounds
Doves, *see* Pigeons
Drews, Herman, 72

Enterprise, Alabama, 91-92
*Exodus*, 35

"Flying foxes," 134-35
Fox hunting, 81-84
Foxhounds, 81-84: description of,
82-84; Goodman, 82-84; homing instincts of, 83-84

Gaul, 51, 100
Geese, 97-101: African, 100;
Chinese, 100; Embden, 98,
100; diet of, 100; Egyptian,
100; mating of, 100; noodling
of, 98; Pilgrim, 100-1; pluck-
ing of, 97-98; for quill pens,
97; species of, 100; and strawberry patches, 101; tempers of,
97-100; Toulouse, 100; White
Roman, 100
Giltz, Dr. M. L., 76
Goats, 27-31: Alpine, 30; characteristics of, 30-31; diet of,
29; intelligence of, 27-28; milk
of, 30; Nubian, 29-30; Saanen,
30; superstitions about, 29;
Toggenburg, 29
Goodman foxhounds, 82-84
Goodpaster, Woodrow, 130-31
Grasshoppers, 33-37: control of,
36; egg-laying of, 34-35; fid-

dling of, 33-34; hearing of, 34;
leap of, 33; long-horned, 35;
plagues of, 35-36, 37; short-
horned, 35; species of, 35
Great horned owls, 109
Guinea fowl, 85-96: characteristics of, 89; description of, 88;
egg-laying of, 89-90; as food,
86-88, 90

Herons, 56
Hinckley Township, Ohio, 69-72
Hoyt, Dr. Sally F., 123-25
Hoyt, Dr. Southgate Y., 122-25

Imperial Valley, California, 74-75
India, bats of, 134-35
Insecticides, 36
Insects, *see* Ants; Grasshoppers;
Weevils

Kingfishers, 56
KMUL, radio station, 24-25

Locusts, 35
Longhorns, *see* Texas longhorns
Los Angeles County Museum, 68
Los Padres National Forest, 66
Louisiana Wild Life and Fisheries
Commission, 58

Malathion, 36
Mammals, *see* Bats; Border col-
lies; Foxhounds; Goats; Mules;
Texas longhorns
Maslowski, Karl, 63-64
*Mayflower*, 43
Mexico, cattle from, 46
Michigan, University of, 15
Missouri mules, 25
Mule Memorial Association, 25
Mules, 21-25: characteristics of,
22-24; Missouri, 25; qualities
of, 21; statue to, 25; types of,
21-22
Muleshoe, Texas, 24-25

Napoleon, 51
Nawalaniec, Walter, 70
*Noctilio*, 134

Ohio Agricultural Experiment
Station, 76
Orioles, 53

*Otus asio, see* Screech owls
Owls, *see* Screech owls; Great
  horned owls

*Paté de foie gras,* 98
Pearson, T. Gilbert, 119
"Peeler," 60-62
Pennsylvania State College, 122
Pigeons, 49-53: breeding of, 53;
  description of, 52-53; incubation of, 53; intelligence of, 53;
  mating of, 53; "milk" of, 53;
  navigation of, 49-51; nesting
  of, 53; species of, 52
Poison ivy, 29

Rabies, 134-35
Raccoons, 56
Red-winged blackbirds, 73-79:
  breeding season of, 77; control
  of, 74-76; 78-79; description of,
  73-74; diet of, 74-76; migra-
  tion of, 77; nesting of, 77-78
Regurgitation, 53, 64, 107-8
Robinson foxhounds, 83
Rock bass, 56
Rock doves, *see* Pigeons
Rome, 51, 100

Santo Domingo, cattle from, 43
Schnierla, Dr. T.C., 112-14, 117-
  18
Screech owls, 103-9: in captivity,
  104-6; description of, 103-4;
  diet of, 104-6; eggs of, 108;
  flight of, 106; hearing of, 106-7;
  noises of, 104; parenthood of,
  108-9; sight of, 106-7; super-
  stitions about, 108; voice of,
  108
Sheep, herding of, 39-42
Shellfish, *see* Crawfish
Sonar, 132
South America, bats of, 133-34
Soybeans, 92
Spraying, 36
Stager, Dr. Kenneth E., 68-69
Steers, herding of, 42
Strawberries, weeding of, 101

Swallows, Capistrano, 70
Texas longhorns, 43-48: auctions
  of, 47; description of, 47-48;
  preservation of, 46-47
Turkey vultures, 63-64; banding
  of, 64; description of, 64; olfactory sense of, 68-69
Turkeys, 88

Vampires, 134
Villalobos, Gregorio de, 43
Vireos, red-eyed, 14, 16-18; feeding of, 17-18
Vultures: Black, 64-65; diet of,
  67; flight of, 66-67; migration
  of, 69-72; nesting of, 72; olfactory sense of, 67-69; protection
  of, 67; sight of, 67-68; taste
  sense of, 69; Turkey, 63-64
  (*see also* Black vultures; California condors; Turkey vultures)

Warblers: black-and-white, 15-
  16; yellow, 14-15
Wasps, 34-35
Weevils, cotton boll, 91-96: adult,
  92-93, 95; control of, 95-96;
  economic importance of, 91-92;
  egg-laying of, 94; larvae of,
  94-95; life cycle of, 92-93;
  pupa of, 95; statue to, 91-92
Whitewater Farmer's Protective
  Association, 74
Wichita Mountains National
  Wildlife Refuge, 48
Wichita National Forest and
  Game Preserve, 46
Wild Life and Fisheries Commission, Louisiana, 58
Woodpeckers, pileated, 119-29:
  adaptability of, 120, 127; in
  captivity, 121, 123-25; control
  of, 122; description of, 119-20;
  diet of, 123, 125-26; eggs of,
  126; as game birds, 127; migration of, 127; nesting of, 126;
  power of, 123-25; tongues of,
  126; and utility poles, 121-22;
  young of, 126-27

# ABOUT THE AUTHOR

George Laycock is well qualified to write about animals, for he grew up on a farm near Zanesville, Ohio, and studied wildlife management at Ohio State University. Mr. Laycock's college career was interrupted for three and a half years of Army service, including twenty months in Europe, where he was commissioned. He then returned to Ohio State to earn his BS in wildlife management in 1947.

During his senior year Mr. Laycock became interested in journalism, and wrote some free-lance magazine articles. One of the magazines for which he wrote was *Farm Quarterly*, and after graduation he joined the staff as associate editor, a post he held for four and a half years. He resigned in 1951 to devote his full time to writing.

Since that time, Mr. Laycock has written numerous articles for such magazines as *Country Gentleman, Sports Illustrated, Better Homes and Gardens, Field and Stream, Outdoor Life, Nature, Sports Afield*, and many others. Several of his articles have been illustrated by his own photographs, and in the course of his research Mr. Laycock has traveled over much of North and South America, observing animals in their natural habitat. He has also written several books, among them the *Deer Hunter's Bible* and *Sign of the Flying Goose*. Laycock lives with his wife and three children in Cincinnati, Ohio.